KENT
CHRISTMAS
A NEW SELECTION

A
KENT
CHRISTMAS
A NEW SELECTION

COMPILED BY

GEOFF & FRAN DOEL

The History Press

First published 2009

The History Press
The Mill, Brimscombe Port
Stroud, Gloucestershire, GL5 2QG
www.thehistorypress.co.uk

British Library Cataloguing in Publication Data.
A catalogue record for this book is available from the British Library.

ISBN 978 0 7524 4892 3

Typesetting and origination by The History Press
Printed in Great Britain

Contents

ACKNOWLEGEMENTS

Thanks to David Hicks, Kevin Bonner-Williams and Malcolm Ward for information on the Westerham Play of the Seven Champions and for invitation and transport to the very enjoyable Ravensbourne Morris Apple Wassailing Night at The Fox Inn Keston, which included the Mummers Play and a Hooden Horse. Thanks to the Ravensbourne Morris/Mummers for permission to use their text of the Westerham Play in this book.

Thanks to Alan and Judy Schneider for prints.

Thanks for information, discussion, performances etc. to Alan Austen, Mick Lynn, Richard Maylam & the Tonbridge Mummers & Hoooeners.

Thanks to the Kent Archaeological Society, the Maidstone Museum, the English Folk Dance & Song Society, and Isobel Doel & the National Trust for assistantance

INTRODUCTION

In pre-Christian times there were midwinter festivities and rituals linked around the solstice, notably the Scandinavian and Germanic festival of Yule, which involved great feasting and which is highly likely to have been celebrated in Anglo-Saxon England. The Catholic Church deliberately targeted such festivals by adopting the 25 December as the date for celebrating Christ's nativity. Many of the old midwinter rituals involving sympathetic magic to restart the growing season, to restore the sun's strength and to continue the life cycle were absorbed into the yearly celebrations of Christ's life cycle, with his birth being celebrated anew each year. Thus the old seasonal pattern of belief was retained in a new form and the iconography and practices of our Christmas and New Year celebrations are a blend of pagan and Christian. Many secular observances have remained. The wassail songs did not invoke Christ's birth, but celebrated food and alcohol and invoked good health for the coming year. Many Boxing Day and New Year traditions have scant direct links with Christianity. So we have an astonishing variety of customs, practices and songs to celebrate.

Even within the Christian tradition there is inconsistency as to the duration of Christmas. For the past 300 years the mysterious Twelve Days of Christmas have defined the festival, though in the past 100 years the festivities have tended to peter out soon after New Year's Day in Kent, rather than ending on the high of a Twelfth Night party. Most of us though remove our decorations on Twelfth Night or Twelfth Day. But in the seventeenth century and earlier, many communal celebrations (such as at courts, castles, and those of some academic and civic institutions) ended, as we shall see in this collection, at Candlemass (2 February). In Roman Catholic times, this long celebration was more or less framed by the twin periods of austerity, Advent and Lent. We have begun and ended our collection with superb poems by the fifteenth-century Canterbury friar, John Ryman, in which he allegorises Advent and Lent as enemies. The first poem dismisses Advent and looks forward to Christmas cheer; the second sadly bids farewell to the festivities in a great hall and forlornly mentions oncoming Lent.

Our first selection of *A Kent Christmas,* published in 1990, sold about 23,000 copies. We have come across enough extra material in this culturally fascinating county to more than justify a second selection.

In this new collection, we have tried to indicate the richness and versatility of the Kent tradition, by giving examples of midwinter celebrations and from earliest Christian times to the present day, looking at Christian and secular, rich and poor, literary and factual. If you enjoy reading this collection half as much as we have enjoyed putting it together, we shall be well rewarded. Wassail!

A KENT CHRISTMAS

From A Canterbury Friar's Advent Poem

BY JOHN RYMAN

The Christmas festivities were preceded, before the Reformation, by the austerities of Advent, a kind of mini Lent in which fish ('styinking fisshe not wortha lowce' and 'plaices thynne') replaced meat in the diet right up to and including Christmas Eve. That it was not just laymen who resented this austerity and longed for Yuletide is shown in this poem by the Canterbury friar, John Ryman. Ryman said he was born in the Weald and his birthplace is thought to be Tenterden. Ryman personifies Advent in his poem, much as Lent was also personified, and indeed in Norwich an actor played the part of Lent being driven out of the city. Ryman wryly consigns Advent to Boughton Blean, out of sight from Canterbury and at the bottom of a big hill. There seems to be an in-joke operating here against Boughton, which might be a general Canterbury attitude or religious rivalry:

Greyfriars, Canterbury. (Geoff Doel)

Fare wele advent, christmas is cume,
Fare wele fro us both alle and sume.

With paciens thou hast us fedde [paciens = 'patience']
And made us go hungrie to bedde:
For lak of mete we were nyghe dedde.
Fare wele fro us both alle and sume.

While thou hast been within oure howse
We ete no puddyngis ne now sawce,
But styinking fisshe not worth a lowce
Fare wele fro us both alle and sume.

Thou hast us fedde with plaices thynne,
Nothing on them but bone and skynne;

Therefore our love thou shalt not wynne,
Fare wele fro us both alle and sume.

Above alle things thou art a meane
To make oure chekes both bare and leane;
I wolde thou were at Boughton Bleane.
Fare wele fro us both alle and sume.

Come thou namore here nor in Kent;
For iff thou doo, thou shalt be shent; [shent = 'shed']
It is ynough to faste in Lent.
Fare wele fro us both alle and sume.

Thou maist not dwell with labouring man;
For on thy fare no skill he can;
For he must ete bothe now and then.
Farewele fro us both alle and sume.

This tyme of Christes feest natal [feest natal = 'nativity']
We will be mery, grete and small,
And thou shalt goo oute of the halle
Fare wele fro us both alle and sume.

Advent is gone. Christmas is cume,
Be we mery now alle and sume;
He is not wise that will be dume,
IN ORTU REGIS OMNIUM ['at the birth of the Lord
   of all']

The First Kent Christmas

No one knows when and where the first Christmas was celebrated in Kent, or even when Christianity was introduced into the county, though a second-century date is suggested, when Britain was still under Roman occupation. The first known English King to receive Christian baptism was Ethelbert of Kent, who rebuilt the ruined Roman city of Canterbury and made it his capital. The kings of Kent subsequently maintained a palace here and had royal interment. In AD 583 or 584, while still a pagan and with a royal lineage which claimed descent from Hengist, Ethelbert married a Christian Frankish princess, Bertha, the daughter of Charibert, King of Paris. Bertha was sent over to Kent accompanied by her chaplain, Liudhard, Bishop of Senlis, and he and his party of monks were given a ruined Roman building outside the Roman city walls to repair and use as a church. This is today the church of Saint Martin at Canterbury, and tradition has it that it was selected because Christians of an earlier period may have worshipped there. Ethelbert reigned for many years and must have joined his wife in the various feast days associated with the celebration of Christ's birth – the Feast of the Nativity on 25 December; and Epiphany, the showing of the Christ child to the Three Kings on 6 January. Later, Christian Kentish kings and their courts would have prepared for Christmas with Advent, a penitential season like

St Martin's Church, Canterbury.

Lent. The season originally consisted of six Sundays beginning on Advent Sunday, the Sunday following St Andrew's Day (30 November), which was considered to be the first day of the Christian year and contained the feast days of the midwinter saints, St Nicholas (later to become our Santa Claus), St Stephen, St Thomas and St Lucy. The decorating of the houses with greenery, the yule log, the mistletoe and midwinter feasting may all have been present in pre-Christian Kent as part of the great pagan midwinter festival which was celebrated throughout northern Europe.

From *The Canterbury Tales*

BY GEOFFREY CHAUCER

In the religious houses, cathedrals and churches, Christmas was celebrated, but the big secular midwinter celebration was New Year and the two were linked together in a festival extending through the Twelve Days of Christmas. In this extract, Chaucer personifies the classical god Janus, from whom the month of January is named, sitting before a fire drinking a huge bumper of wine and eating pork; this secular image is combined with cries of 'Noel', relating to the joy at the Nativity. Janus has a double beard because he has two faces, one looking back at the past year, one looking forward into the new year. This image neatly reflects the dual attitude to New Year which survives right through to the present day, when we look back at our past experiences in the year just ended and survey our hopes for the coming year.

'The Franklin's Tale' is both a celebration of married love (a conclusion to Chaucer's celebrated marriage debate running through several of *The Canterbury Tales*) and a Breton Lay dramatically testing the chivalric concept of truth. The virtuous wife Dorigen has given a rash promise to a young squire, Aurelius, seeking her love that she will indulge his passion if he can remove the rocks from the Breton coast which she sees as a threat to her husband's safety. Arelius seeks the help of a

Geoffrey Chaucer, from an early manuscript.

magician-astrologer, hence the several astrological allusions in this midwinter passage:

> And this was, as thise bookes me remember,
> The colde frosty season of Decembre,
> Phebus wax old, and hewed like latoun
> (the sun was near setting and coloured like brass)
> That in his hote declinacioun (zenith)
> Shone as the burned gold with stremes brighte.
> But now in Capricorn adown he lighte
> Where as he shone full pale, I dare well sayn:
> The bitter frostes with the sleet and rain
> Destroyed hath the green in every yerd.
> Janus sit by the fire with double beerd
> And drinketh of his bugle horn the win,
> Biforn him stant brawen of the tusked swin,
> (Before him stands meat of the wild boar),
> And 'Nowell!' crieth every lusty man.

From 'The Seven Poor Travellers'
BY CHARLES DICKENS

The last section of 'The Seven Poor Travellers', which is entitled 'The Road', starts off with 'the delights of a Kentish ramble in the winter.' Dickens had been a great walker all his life and was particularly alive to the beauties of Kent. One local man had noted that, 'Dickens was

Cobham Hall.

a smoker, he liked a pipe, a good cigar more, soon after breakfast or dinner, but I never saw him smoke either pipe or cigar when out walking. On the road it was walk, walk, walk, at a fast pace. He knew every church and churchyard for miles'.

The palpable Christian sentiment with which 'The Seven Poor Travellers' ends reminds us that Dickens was a man of religious sensibility with a particular interest in the New Testament – he had for example written *The Life of Our Lord* primarily for his own children, but which he later had published. Peter Ackroyd, in his biography of Dickens, thinks that there is a disparity between the 'vigorous public expression of Christian sentiment' promulgated in his Christmas books and 'his almost total lack of interest in Christian sentiment or Christian representatives… his beliefs were determined by his own vision of the world rather than by any inherited or specific creed.' This may be so but Dickens was known to have attended Shorne Church on a regular basis while resident at Gad's Hill and it may also be, as a contemporary schoolteacher living at Rochester remarked, that 'Dickens was more religiously inclined than many would suppose':

I was going to walk, by Cobham Woods, as afar upon my way to London…When I came to the style and footpath by which I was to diverge from the main-road, I bade farewell to my last remaining Poor Traveller, and pursued my way alone. And now, the mists began to rise in the most beautiful manner, and the sun to shine; and as I went on through the bracing air, seeing the hoar-frost sparkle everywhere I felt as though all Nature shared in the joy of the great Birthday.

Going through the woods, the softness of my tread upon the mossy ground and among the brown leaves, enhanced the Christmas sacredness by which I felt surrounded. As the whitened stems environed me, I thought how the Founder of the time had never raised his benignant hand, save to bless and heal, except in the case of one unconscious tree. By Cobham Hall, I came to the village and the churchyard where the dead had been quietly buried, 'in the sure and certain hope' which Christmas time inspired. What children could I see at play, and not be loving of, recalling who had loved them. No garden that I passed was out of unison with the day, for I remembered that the tomb was in a garden, and that 'she, supposing him to be the gardener' had said 'Sir, if thou have borne him hence, tell me where thou hast laid him, and I will take him away.' In time, the distant river with the ships, came full in view and with it picture of the poor fishermen mending their nets, who arose and followed him- of the teaching of the people from a ship pushed off a little way from shore, by reason of the multitude - of a majestic figure, for did not the people lay their sick where the mere shadows of the men who had heard and seen him, might fall as they passed along?

Thus, Christmas begirt me, far and near, until I had come to Blackheath, and had walked down the long vista of gnarled old trees in Greenwich Park, and was being stream-rattled, through the mists now closing in once more, towards the lights of London. Brightly they shone, but not so brightly as my own fire and the brighter faces around it, when we came together to celebrate the day.

'While Shepherds Watched Their Flocks by Night'
BY NAHUM TATE

Words by Nahum Tate to the tune of 'Cranbrook' by Thomas Clarke.

West Galley choirs (or quires) with stringed instruments sometimes augmented with serpents, clarinets and oboes were popular in Kent in the eighteenth and early

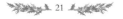

nineteenth centuries and featured locally written carols and tunes. This was one of the consequences of the Puritan assault on church services and church music, the creation of 'homemade' music played by parishioners for whom wooden west galleries were built usually adjacent to the towers, hence the name West Galley Music. The standard of these musicians, plus child and sometimes adult choristers, was often very high and they composed sacred songs and set psalms and biblical paraphrases to

An old print of a church choir.

'While Shepherds Watched Their Flocks by Night' to the tune of Cranbrook by Thomas Clark.

new tunes, arranged for instrumental and vocal harmonic forms. The most popular work to be so set was Nahum Tate's 'While Shepherds Watched Their Flocks by Night', and scores of fine tunes and harmonic settings for this are found throughout England. One of the finest Kent composers and West Gallery musicians was the Canterbury shoemaker Thomas Clark and his tune, known as 'Cranbrook', was later used for the Yorkshire 'national anthem', 'On Ilkley Moor Ba Tat'.

Biddenden had a choir of singers, accompanied by bass viol and clarinet until 1850, and William Tarbutt

Rochester Christmas crib. (Archie Turnbull)

of Cranbrook remembered the choir going out on
Christmas morning round the village singing 'While
Shepherds Watched'. Frittenden had a celebrated band
that toured the village playing carols on Christmas Eve,
featuring bass drum, flugel horn, two cornets, French
horn, trombone, uphonium, tuba and side-drum.

> While shepherds watched their flocks by night.
> The Angel of the Lord came down,
> And glory shone around.
>
> 'Fear not', said he. For mighty dread
> Had seized their troubled mind.
> 'Glad tidings of great joy I bring
> To you and all mankind.

To you in David's town this day
Is born of David's line
A saviour who is Christ the Lord
And this shall be a sign.
'The heavenly babe you there shall find
To human view displayed
All meanly wrapped in swaddling bands
And in a manger laid.'

Thus spake the seraph and forthwith
Appeared a shining throng
Of angels praising God who thus
Addressed their joyful song.

All glory be to God on high
And to the earth be peace.
Good will henceforth from heaven to men
Begin and never cease.

Tudor Christmases at Greenwich, 1486 and 1513

From *The Palace and the Hospitals – Or Chronicles of Greenwich, 1886* and *Hall's Chronicle*.

Greenwich had a long tradition as a Royal palace, and had been owned by Edward IV, whose Queen is mentioned

in the text as dining with her son-in-law, Henry VII, who is said to have imprisoned her at Bermondsey Nunnery. It should be remembered that Elizabeth, as a Yorkist, was on a different side in the Wars of the Roses to Henry Tudor, even though Richard III, who reigned between her husband and Henry, was responsible for the killing of two of her sons, the 'princes in the tower'. Henry had to initially treat Elizabeth with some caution and placing her in a nunnery was a conventional way of dealing with the problem of the widows of opponents. However, Henry's enlightened idea of uniting the houses of Lancaster and York by marrying Elizabeth's daughter, the Yorkist heiress, enabled a reconciliation of which this dinner is an example. The Queen was also at Greenwich in December 1489.

There is an interesting description of the New Year custom of 'crying out' the full list of all the titles of the King and the leading nobles present:

Here (Greenwich) the king kept Christmas this year, and went to the Mass of the Virgin in a rich gown of purple velvet, furred with sables. On Christmas Day he sat at dinner in the great chamber and the queen and her mother in the queen's chamber. This distinction is to be marked, inasmuch as it has been said that the late queen (Elizabeth Woodville) was kept in prison by Henry in a nunnery at Bermondsey. He seems to have deprived her of Greenwich and her other property, but we find her here dining with the queen, though not in public.

On New Year's Day there was a noisy ceremony here. The king was cried in his style accustomed – that is, all

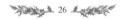

The Lord of Misrule, taken from 'Old Christmas Customs'.

possible titles that he could be given were called out, and at the end the significant word 'Largess!' was shouted. Not only the king, but all the nobility above barons, except ecclesiastics, were similarly honoured and mulcted. At night, on this day, there was, we read, 'goodly disguising;' there had been 'divers plays' at Christmas. On Twelfth Night, the king and queen sat down according to custom at a grand banquet. The Earl of Ormond (Lord Rochford) was Queen's Chamberlain. After the second course, the minstrels played, and the officers of arms descended, and the Garter King thanked the King for his largess; they then cried 'Largess' again. The king sat under a canopy, wearing a jewelled golden crown, and the queen under another, a little lower on the left; the Archbishop of Canterbury sat on the king's right hand at the high table. The table, which was on the right side of the hall, was for gentlemen; the Duke of Bedford began it, and the French ambassador sat next him. The table on the left was for ladies, and was begun by the queen's sister, Lady Cecil. In those days, men of rank thought it a high honour to perform menial duties on great occasions; and on this one, the Earl of Oxford waited on the king, while the Earl of Ormond knelt to the queen. Sir David Owen was carver, and Sir Charles cup-bearer, Sir William Vampage was sewer, that is he wore a towel, and put on and took off the dishes; and Sir John Furtzen waited at the cupboard (side-board) in a gown of crimson velvet, with a collar round his neck. At a table in the middle of the hall sat the dean and those of the king's chapel who, after the first course, sang a 'choral'.

Henry VIII continued his father's practice of celebrating Christmas in magnificent style at Greenwich. This is Hall's description of Henry's spectacular Twelfth Night Masque, which ended the festivities of Christmas 1513 and was held in the Great Hall before Queen Catherine of Arragon, and the court. The artificial hill (the riche mount) appears to have been used year after year as it is referred to as an 'olde custom' and was probably wheeled into the Great Hall and stabilised. No indication is given as to how the beacon (bekon) was lit up. Although it is not mentioned, musicians would have been entertaining the company all evening and the final dance would have proceeded at a stately pace in order for everyone to admire the gorgeous clothes as well as the young King's acclaimed dancing skills:

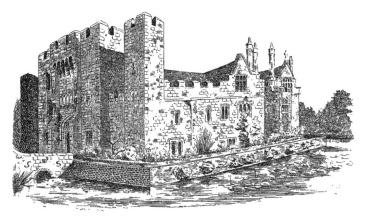

Hever Castle.

According to olde custom there came into the greate hall
a mount called the riche mount. This mount was set full
of riche flowers of silk, and especially of brome slippes full
of poddes, the branches were greene satin, and the flowers
flat gold damaske, which signified Plantaganet; on the top
stood a goodly bekon giving light, rounde above the bekon
sat the King and five others, al in coates and capes of right
crimosin velvet, embroidered with flat gold of damaske,
their coats set full of spangells of gold; and foure wood-
houses drew the mount till it came before the Queen and
then the King and his compaigne descended and daunced;
then suddenly the mount opened and out came six ladies
all in crimosin satin and plunket, embroidered with golde
and perle, with French hoodes on their heddes, and they
daunced alone. Then the lordes of the mount took the

ladies and daunced together, and the ladies re-entered, and
the mount closed, and so was conveyed out of the hall.

The Twelve Days of Christmas over 1527-28 was a far
less happy occasion for Catherine, although it was as
usual being celebrated with much pomp at Greenwich.
In the midst of the Christmas festivities and out of the
blue the disease known as 'the sweating sickness' had
reappeared in Kent. Characteristically the illness, which
was viewed as a kind of plague, began with cold shivers followed by severe headaches and giddiness. Then
came pains throughout the body, but in particular the
neck, shoulders and limbs. This stage lasted from half an
hour's to three or four hours. After that came an excess
of sweating and the experience of intense heat. At this
stage, the patient began to experience headaches, diso-
rientation, heart palpitations, a rapid pulse and intense
thirst. With the last stage came an irresistible urge to
go to sleep, though some went into total collapse. The
French Ambassador to the English Court wrote 'this disease is the easiest in the world to die of. You have a slight
plain in the head and at the heart; all at once you begin
to sweat. There is no need for a physician…you are
taken off without languishing.' Henry VIII was known
to be personally terrified of this mysterious and highly
virulent viral disease whose cause was unknown and
for which no cure had been found. Under normal circumstances, Henry would have cancelled the Christmas
activities and moved his entourage all round the country. This time he did not, for he was in love with one

of his Queen's ladies in waiting – Anne Boleyn – and either she or one of her personal servants had fallen sick with the sweating sickness in her family home at Hever Castle, where the Boleyn family had decided to remain until the sickness had burnt itself out. Now Henry paid her marked attention, quitting the Twelve Days of Christmas entertainments provided at court and riding over from Greenwich to Hever almost every day. It was said that he gave notice of his approach by the sounding of a horn from 'King Harry's Hill'. A series of love letters (the earliest were written in French) have been discovered from this date from Henry to Anne and charter the warmth of his feelings, as well as Anne's skills at keeping him at arm's length. This letter is thought to date to this time:

> In debating with myself the contents of your letters I have been put to a great agony, not knowing how to understand them, whether to my disadvantage as shown in some places, or to my advantage as in others, I beseech you now with all my heart definitely to let me know your whole mind as to the love between us; for necessity compels me to plague you for a reply, having been for more than a year now struck by the dart of love, and being uncertain either of failure or of finding a place in your heart and affection, which point has certainly kept me for some time from naming you as my mistress, since if you only love me with an ordinary love the name is not appropriate to you, seeing that it stands for an uncommon position very remote from the ordinary, but if it pleases you to do the duty of a true, loyal

mistress and friend, and to give yourself body, and heart to me, who have been, and will be, your very loyal servant (if your rigour does not forbid me), I promise you that not only the name will be due to you, but also to take you as my sole mistress, casting off all others, than yourself out of mind and affection, and to serve you only, begging you to make me a complete reply to this my rude letter as to how far and in what I can trust, and if it does not please you to reply in writing, to let me know of some place where I can have it by word or mouth, the which place I will seek out with all my heart. No more for fear of wearying you.

Written by the hand of him who would willingly remain yours.

HR

Christmas Charities – Thomasing & Goodening

Charitable bequests in pre-Reformation days were ways in which donors could acquire spiritual merit on and after their deaths, thus being able to mitigate the longs spells in Purgatory which the Roman Catholic religion believed intervened between death and elevation to heaven. The practice did continue throughout the sixteenth century, and many Kent churches have display boards giving details of defunct, and in a few cases of surviving, charitable bequests. However, there was a marked decline in the seventeenth century, when Puritan rectors were opposed to the continuance of practices which they felt adhered to outmoded Romanish beliefs. The pious nineteenth century led to a new spate of charitable foundations and bequests and the more scrupulous administration of existing ones; some practices which the Victorians felt to be unseemly in a religious context, such as the distribution of beer in the church (or indeed of beer at all) were revised. Thus each age modifies custom according to its own beliefs and prejudices. As well as the endowed bequests, there were a number of less formal, yearly handouts to the poor, unendowed, but usually with a traditional benefactor, family, or group of benefactors. The most appropriate seasons of the church calendar for such distributions, formal and informal, were Easter (with its associations with 'maunds' and Christ's instructions to look after the poor) and Advent, particularly St Thomas's Day, where money or food could be given towards the celebration of Christmas.

The St Thomas Day (21 December) charities reflect active, but traditionally expected, begging, particularly on the part of widows; it is variously known in Kent as 'gooding', 'goodening', 'mumping' and 'dawdlin'. This Advent custom is conveniently placed for collection largesse for the Christmas celebrations, but the traditional Kentish explanation for the date is that St Thomas had to pay for doubting the resurrection of Christ and the custom commemorates this. In reality, in Roman Catholic days, dating of significant or festive events was often by using saints' days. By the early nineteenth century, the survival of gooding was strongest in the villages around Maidstone. William Hone's *Every Day Book* of 1825 comments on the survival of the custom at Loose, Linton and Barming:

> At Loose, Mr T Charlton gives the poor of the parish certain quantities of wheat, apportioned to their families, in addition to which, his daughters give the widows a new flannel petticoat each, who at the same time, go to the other respectable inhabitants of the place to solicit the usual donatory, and it is not an uncommon thing for a family to get in this way six or seven shillings…the custom is also prevalent at Linton an adjoining parish; and I am also informed that Lord Cornwallis, who resides there, intends giving to the resident poor something very considerable. At Barming, C Whittaker, Esq is provided with one hundred loaves to distribute to the resident poor on this day, which to my knowledge is annual on his part; they likewise go to other respectable inhabitants, who also give their alms in the way they think best.

Alfred Moore, in an article in the *Kentish Gazette* on the subject of 'Goodenin' in April 1895, defines the custom as 'the going round just before Christmas of poor people to the residences of more wealthy neighbours to solicit small gifts of money (occasionally of meal or floor also) the request being generally put in the formula of "Please remember the goodenin" and the doles being goodenin gifts'.

Moore was sent very useful information by 'an old gentleman at Willesbrough' who was a resident and

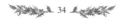

eyewitness of the custom at Leeds in 1845, whence it continued until about 1865. Moore describes the activity at Leeds in 1845 from his informant's notes:

The gooeners (who were either widows or poor women with large families) met at a gate opposite the Ten Bells Inn at ten o'clock on the morning of St Thomas's Day. An old widow who was known as Granny Hicks was chosen 'Queen of the Goodeners', after which election they started on their 'dawdling' as it was then called. The party was under the entire control of its queen, calling only at such houses as she thought proper, the first being to Burgess Hall where Granny made a deep curtsey to Farmer Hodsell with a 'Please remember the goodeners' and was rewarded with a coin of the realm. Crossing the fields and calling at most of the houses, they reached Fulling Mill Farm where Mr Betts gave old Granny half-a-crown and a peck of wheat which was his regular custom. Crossing more fields, the party came out into the Maidstone and Ashford Road and on into the parish of Broomfield to Leeds Castle, where all the goodeners standing together curtsied to the squire, wished him a Merry Christmas and were presented with five shillings, after which they gradually worked their way by another route back to the place from whence they had started, where they arrived at about three o'clock in the afternoon after a perambulation of some six miles or more. The money which had been collected was here shared out, but I regret to say that it only amounted to eight pence for each member of the expedition in which about thirty goodeners took part.

Bread Dole, Cobham Church. (Geoff Doel)

Christmas Bread Dole, Cobham

A board in the nave of St Mary Magdalene Church in Cobham (see photo) records a Christmas charity bequeathed, by the Hayes family of Owletts, a substantial property in the village. William Hayes bequeathed through his will (1678) for the 'Poor of this Parish for ever. TWENTY SHILLINGS (issuing out of his Lands) to be laid out in Bread on Christmas Eve annually.'

In 1789, Richard Hayes bequeathed 'to the Poor of this Parish for the Timebeing (being Householders therein) and not receiving Relief, EIGHTY POUNDS.' Richard's bequest was administered by trustees from investments and it is interesting to note that he wisely stipulated 'for the Timebeing' instead of 'forever'!

The Thrale Christmas Charity, Knockholt

Bequests for Christmas charity were common in the eighteenth and nineteenth centuries, taking over from the St Thomas Day Doles, many of which started before the Reformation. Information on the Thrale Charity is from David Waldron Smithers' *A History of Knockolt* (1991).

Miss Susanna Thrale, the second daughter of the brewer Henry Thrale of Streatham, and Hester Thrale, the friend of Dr Johnson, moved to Ash Cottage, Knockholt about 1819 and died there in 1858 aged eighty-eight. The Hales' Streatham brewery had been sold in 1784 for £135,000.

Susanna Thrale left money in her will for the vicar of Knockolt, the school, five widows and annual provision for Christmas charity.

The Christmas bequest was £50 a year to be distributed for food, warm clothing and books. The bequest was organized through the Charity Commissioners and a Thrale Christmas Charity account book for 1861 still survives. Due to prudent investment the charity is still operating.

Birling Manor

An account of around 1872 records that:

> Gifts were as usual provided for the workmen on the Manor Estate and also for the poorest amongst the villages at Birling, Ham-hill and Ryarsh. Joints of beef of 4lbs and upwards were given for Christmas dinner and gifts of warm clothing, dresses, shawls, stockings, flannel blankets and jerseys were distributed to the needy with a liberal hand, while each widow received additionally a quarter pound of tea. A servant's dance was given at the Manor on the evening of January 6th for the Manor servants and some of the workmen together with a few friends…The members of the Birling band provided excellent music and at 9pm the Hon R.P. Nevill led off the dance with Mrs Bunch, the housekeeper.
>
> Every Christmas the Nevill family gave a party for the village children and everyone returned home with a toy and a garment. The estate workers were given joints of beef for Christmas.

From The Great Inundation

by Nathan Drew

Kent has, in its recent past, suffered greatly from great gales which have inflicted great damage and destruction. This is an early account written down in the nineteenth century but which draws on earlier sources and describes the extensive damage done to property, goods and the loss of life in and around Deptford in the mid-seventeenth century when a series of massive tidal waves swept upriver. Christmas at this date had been abolished by the Puritans, though they had no objection to the celebration of New Year's Day which, in this case, was the last thing on people's minds:

THE GREAT INUNDATION – A terrible storm from the north-east swept over the district on January 1st, 1651, causing an inundation of the Thames of unparalleled magnitude. Deptford suffered greatly. About 2pm the storm became so violent that the waves forced down the piles of wood, and entered the merchant shipping yards, removing great trees and pieces of timber, that twenty horses could scarcely move. By 2.30pm there were seven feet of water in the streets of the Lower Town, which rose three feet more during the next half-hour. Most of the inhabitants fled to the Upper Town, leaving their goods and chattels 'to the mercy,' as the old chronicler states, 'of the merciless waves.' Those inhabitants who did not effect their escape in time

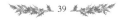

A print of Deptford in the seventeenth century.

had to be rescued by watermen in boats from their chamber windows; some are said to have perished. The flood forced its way into Gammer Farthing's house, who being turning the spit, laden with gallant goose, and having two children, one in the cradle and another out of it, ran forth to call her husband, but before their return, the house was about three feet deep in water; the cradle floating with the child in it; the goose swimming; and the other child saved itself by getting on top of a high table, which sad spectacle the father perceiving, rushed up to the middle in water, and brought forth his two children.' The waters began to subside about 4pm. Besides the damage done to the various shipping yards and dwellings, some two hundred sheep, cows, bullocks, and other cattle were drowned in the Deptford meadows and other fields adjacent. The old chronicler of this event concludes by humbly imploring his readers in the future to bear in record this observation: 'That when you discern the sun to be eclipsed and the appearing of three black clouds, then expect great inundations, loss of cattel, changes and dreadful revolutions, even as a signal from heaven; to purge nations and Commonwealth from oppression and tyranny and to restore the Freeborn their just Freedom and Liberty that so peace may abound within the walls of Sion, and each man enjoy their own again.'

It appears that three black clouds were seen in the firmament at Deptford on the evening preceeding the day of this great flood.

From *Great Expectations*
BY CHARLES DICKENS

Great Expectations opens dramatically on Christmas Eve in Cooling churchyard, with its famous set of children's graves from one family, in the Cooling Marshes of the Hoo peninsula, with the Thames estuary to the north and the Medway estuary to the south. It was a landscape which Dickens was familiar with from his own childhood in Chatham. He describes it as remembered by a child and evokes the atmosphere and terror superbly. The action at the beginning of the story has been estimated by a series of references to take place about 1812, the year of Dickens' birth. Later, Dickens honeymooned in nearby Chalk and then bought Gad's Hill in 1857, from where he would often walk to Cooling.

Later in this extract is a superb evocation of an early nineteenth-century domestic Christmas, with particular reference to the food and drink, some of which Pip has stolen for the convict, leading to the wonderfully comic description of Mr Pumblechook drinking tar-water in mistake for brandy. The action predates the Victorian practice of Christmas presents, but Pip's pretence of having been to hear the carols on Christmas morning is interesting as it doesn't seem to refer to church, which he and Joe go to later in the morning. This may refer to outdoor carols in the manner of Thomas Hardy's family quire as described in *Under the Greenwood Tree*. It is a pity that Dickens only refers to this offstage:

Ours was the marsh country, down by the river, within, as the river wound, twenty miles of the sea. My first most vivid and broad impression of the identity of things, seems to me to have been gained on a memorable raw afternoon towards evening. At such a time I found out for certain, that this bleak place overgrown with nettles was the church-yard; and that Philip Pirrip, late of this parish, and also Georgiana, wife of the above, were dead and buried; and that Alexander, Bartholomew, Abraham, Tobias, and Roger, infant children of the aforesaid, were also dead and buried; and that the dark flat wilderness beyond the churchyard, intersected with dykes and mounds and gates, with scattered cattle feeding on it, was the marshes; and that the low leaden line beyond, was the river; and that the distant savage lair from which the wind was rushing, was the sea; and that the small bundle of shivers growing afraid of it all and beginning to cry, was Pip.

'Hold your noise!' cried a terrible voice, as a man started up from among the graves at the side of the church porch. 'Keep still, you little devil, or I'll cut your throat!'

A fearful man, all in coarse grey, with a great iron on his leg. A man with no hat, and with broken shoes, and with an old rag tied round his head. A man who had been soaked in water, and smothered in mud, and lamed by stones, and cut by flints, and stung by nettles, and torn by briars; who limped, and shivered, and glared and growled; and whose teeth chattered in his head as he seized me by the chin.

'O! Don't cut my throat, sir,' I pleaded in terror. 'Pray don't do it, sir.'

'Tell us your name! said the man. 'Quick!'

'Pip, sir.'

'Once more,' said the man, staring at me. 'Give it mouth!'

'Pip, Pip, sir!

'Show us where you live,' said the man. 'Pint out the place!'

I pointed to where our village lay, on the flat in-shore among the alder-trees and pollards, a mile or more from the church.

The man, after looking at me for a moment, turned me upside-down and emptied my pockets. There was nothing in them but a piece of bread. When the church came to itself - for he was so sudden and strong that he made it go

Gravestones of Cooling Church. (Geoff Doel)

head over heels before me, and I saw the steeple under my feet – when the church came to itself, I say, I was seated on a high tombstone, trembling, while he ate the bread ravenously.

'Now then, lookee here!' said the man. 'Where's your mother?'

'There, sir!' said I.

He started, made a short run, and stopped and looked over his shoulder.

'There, sir!' I timidly explained. 'Also Georgiana. That's my mother.'

'Oh!' said he, coming back. 'And is that your father alonger your mother?'

'Yes, sir,' said I, 'him too; late of this parish.'

'Ha!' he muttered then, considering. 'Who d'ye live with –supposin' you're kindly let to live, which I han't made up my mind about?'

'My sister, sir – Mrs Joe Gargery – wife of Joe Gargery, the blacksmith, sir.'

'Blacksmith, eh?' said he. And looked down at his leg.

After darkly looking at his leg and at me several times, he came closer to my tombstone, took me by both arms, and tilted me back as far as he could hold me; so that his eyes looked most powerfully down into mine, and mine looked most helplessly up into his.

'Now lookee here,' he said, 'the question being whether you're to be let to live. You know what a file is.'

'Yes, sir.'

'And you know what wittles is.'

'Yes sir.'

After each question he tilted me over a little more, so as to give me a greater sense of helplessness and danger.

'You get me a file.' He tilted me again. 'And you get me wittles.' He tilted me again. 'Or I'll have your heart and liver out.' He tilted me again. 'You bring me, to-morrow morning early, that file and them wittles. You bring the lot to me, at that old Battery over yonder. You do it, and you never dare to say a word or dare to make a sign concern-ing your having seen such a person as me, or any person sumever, and you shall be let to live. You fail, or you go from my words in any partickler, no matter how small it is, and your heart and your liver shall be tore out, roasted and ate. Now, I ain't alone, as you may think I am. There's a young man hid with me, in comparison with which young man I am an Angel. That young man hears the words I speak. That young man has a secret way pecooliar to himself, of getting at a boy, and at his heart, and at his liver. It is in wain for a boy to attempt to hide himself from that young man. A boy may lock his door, maybe warm in bed, may tuck himself up, may draw the clothes over his head, may think himself comfortable and safe, but that young man will softly creep and creep his way to him and tear him open. I am a keeping that young man from harming of you at the present moment, with great difficulty. I find it wery hard to hold that young man off your inside. Now, what do you say?'

I said that I would get him the file, and I would get him what broken bits of food I could, and I would come to him at the Battery early in the morning.

'Say Lord strike you dead if you don't!' said the man.

I said so and he took me down.

'Now,' he pursued, 'you remember what you've undertook, and you remember that young man, and you get home!'

'Goo-good night, sir,' I faltered.

'Much of that!' said he, glancing about him over the cold wet flat. 'I wish I was a frog. Or a eel!'

At the same time, he hugged his shuddering body in both his arms – clasping himself, as if to hold himself together – and limped towards the low church wall. As I saw him go, picking his way among the nettles, and among the brambles that bound the green mounds, he looked in my young eyes as if he were eluding the hands of the dead people, stretching up cautiously out of their graves, to get a twist upon his ankle and pull him in.

When he came to the low church wall, he got over it, like a man whose legs were numbed and stiff, and then turned round to look for me. When I saw him turning, I set my face towards home, and made the best use of my legs. But presently I looked over my shoulder, and saw him going on again towards the river, still hugging himself in both arms, and picking his way with his sore feet among the great stones dropped into the marshes here and there,

Dickens' honeymoon cottage, Chalk. (Geoff Doel)

for stepping-places when the rains were heavy, or the tide was in.

The marshes were just a long black horizontal line then, as I stopped to look after him; and the river was just another horizontal line, not nearly so broad nor yet so black; and the shy was just a row of long angry red lines and dense black lines intermixed. On the edge of the river I could faintly make out the only two black things in all the prospect that seemed to be standing upright; one of these was the beacon by which the sailors steered – like an unhooped cask upon a pole – an ugly thing when you were near it; the other, a gibber with some chains hanging to it which had once held a pirate. The man was limping towards this latter, as if he were the pirate come to life, and come down, and going back to hook himself up again. It gave me a terrible turn when I thought so; and as I saw the cattle lifting their heads to gaze after him, I wondered whether they thought so too. I looked all round for the horrible young man, and could see no signs of him. But, now I was frightened again, and ran home without stopping.

It was Christmas Eve, and I had to stir the pudding for the next day, with a copper-stick, from seven to eight by the Dutch clock.

'Hark!' said I when I had done my stirring, and was taking a final warm in the chimney corner before being sent up to bed; 'was that great guns, Joe?'

'Ah!' said Joe. 'There's another conwict off.'

'What does that mean, Joe?' said I.

Mrs. Joe, who always took explanations upon herself, said, snappishly, 'Escaped. Escaped.' Administering the definition like Tar-water.

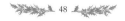

While Mrs. Joe sat with her head bending over her nee-
dlework, I put my mouth into the forms of saying to Joe,
'What's a convict?' Joe put *his* mouth into the forms of
returning such a highly elaborate answer, that I could make
out nothing of it but the single word 'Pip'. 'There was a
conwict off last night,' said Joe, aloud, 'after sunset-gun.
And they fired warning of him. And now, it appears they're
firing warning of another.'

'*Who's* firing?' said I.

'Drat that boy,' interposed my sister, frowning at me over
her work, 'what a questioner he is. Ask no questions, and
you'll be told no lies.'

'Mrs Joe…I should like to know…where the firing
comes from?'

'Lord bless the boy!' exclaimed my sister, as if she didn't
quite mean that, but rather the contrary. 'From the Hulks.'

'And please what's Hulks?' said I.

'That's the way with this boy!' exclaimed my sister, pointing me out with her needle and thread, and shaking her head
at me. 'Answer him one question, and he'll ask you a dozen
directly. Hulks are prison-ships, right 'cross th' meshes.' We
always used that name for marshes, in our country.

'I wonder who's put into prison-ships, and why they're put
there?' said I, in a general way, and with quiet desperation.

It was too much for Mrs Joe, who immediately rose. 'I
tell you what, young fellow,' said she, 'I didn't bring you
up by hand to badger people's lives out…People are put
in the Hulks because they murder, and because they rob,
and forge, and do all sorts of bad; and they always begin by
asking questions. Now, you get along to bed!'

I was never allowed a candle to light me to bed, and, as I went upstairs in the dark, with my head tingling – from Mrs Joe's thimble, having played the tambourine upon it, to accompany her last words – I felt fearfully sensible of the great convenience that the Hulks were handy for me. I was clearly on my way there. I had begun by asking questions, and I was going to rob Mrs Joe.

As soon as the great velvet pall outside my little window was shot with grey, I got up and went downstairs; every board upon the way, and every crack in every board, calling after me, 'Stop thief!' and 'Get up, Mrs Joe!' In the pantry, which was far more abundantly supplied than usual, owing to the season, I was very much alarmed, by a hare hanging up by the heels, whom I rather thought I caught, when my back was half turned, winking…I stole some bread, some rind of cheese, about half a jar of mincemeat (which I tied up in my pocket-handkerchief with my last night's slice), some brandy from a stone bottle (which I decanted into a glass bottle I had secretly used for making that intoxicating fluid, Spanish-liquorice-water, up in my room: diluting the stone bottle from a jug in the kitchen cupboard), a meat bone with very little on it, and a beautiful round compact pork pie. I was nearly going away without the pie, but I was tempted to mount upon a shelf, to look what it was that was put away so carefully in a covered earthenware dish in a corner, and I found it .was the pie, and I took it, in the hope that it was not intended for early use, and would not be missed for some time.

There was a door in the kitchen, communicating with the forge; I unlocked and unbolted that door, and got a

Joe Gargery's forge, Cooling. (Geoff Doel)

file from among Joe's tools. Then, I put the fastenings as I had found them, opened the door at which I had entered when I ran home last night, shut it, and ran for the misty marshes.

(Joe gives the food to the escaped convict Magwitch and also catches a glimpse of a second convict. He then returns home for the Christmas festivities.)

I fully expected to find a Constable in the kitchen, waiting to take me up. But not only was there no Constable there, but no discovery had yet been made of the robbery. Mrs Joe was prodigiously busy in getting the house ready for the festivities of the day, and Joe had been put upon the kitchen door-step to keep him out of the dustpan – an arti-

cle into which his destiny always led him sooner or later, when my sister was vigorously reaping the floors of her establishment.

'And where the deuce ha' *you* been?' was Mrs Joe's Christmas salutation, when I and my conscience showed ourselves.

I said I had been down to hear the Carols. 'Ah! well!' observed Mrs Joe. 'You might ha' done worse.' Not a doubt of that, I thought.

'Perhaps if I warn't a blacksmith's wife, and (what's the same thing) a slave with her apron never off *I* should have been to hear the Carols,' said Mrs Joe. 'I'm rather partial to Carols, myself, and that's the best of reasons for my never hearing any.'

We were to have a superb dinner, consisting of a leg of pickled pork and greens, and a pair of roast stuffed fowls. A handsome mince-pie had been made yesterday morning (which accounted for the mincemeat not being missed), and the pudding was already on the boil. These extensive arrangements occasioned us to be cut off unceremoniously in respect of breakfast; 'for I an't,' said Mrs Joe, 'I an't a going to have no formal cramming and busting and washing up now, with what I've got before me, I promise you!

So we had our slices served out, as if we were two thousand troops on a forced march instead of a man and boy at home; and we took gulps of milk and water, with apologetic countenances, from a jug on the dresser. In the mean time, Mrs Joe put clean white curtains up, and tacked a new flowered-flounce across the wide chimney to replace the old one, and uncovered the little state parlour across the passage, which was never uncovered at any other time, but passed the rest of the year in a cool haze of silver paper, which even extended to the four little white crockery poodles on the mantelshelf, each with a black nose and a basket of flowers in his mouth, and each the counterpart of the other. Mrs Joe was a very clean housekeeper, but had an exquisite art of making her cleanliness more uncomfortable and unacceptable than dirt itself. Cleanliness is next to Godliness, and some people do the same by their religion.

My sister having so much to do, was going to church vicariously; that is to say, Joe and I were going. In his working clothes, Joe was a well-knit characteristic-looking blacksmith; in his holiday clothes, he was more like a scarecrow in good circumstances, than anything else. Nothing that he wore then, fitted him or seemed to belong to him; and everything that he wore then, grazed him. On the present festive occasion he emerged from his room, when the blithe bells were going, the picture of misery, in a full suit of Sunday penitentials. As to me…I was always treated as if I had insisted on being born, in opposition to the dictates of reason, religion, and morality, and against the dissuading arguments of my best friends. Even when I was taken to have a new suit of clothes, the tailor had orders to make them like a kind of Reformation, and on no account to let me have the free use of my limbs.

Joe and I going to church, therefore, must have been a moving spectacle for compassionate minds. Yet, what I suffered outside, was nothing to what I underwent within. The terrors that had assailed me whenever Mrs Joe had gone near the pantry, or out of the room, were only to be equalled by the remorse with which my mind dwelt on what my hands had done.

I conceived the idea that the time when the banns were read and when the clergyman said, 'Ye are now to declare it!' would be the time for me to rise and propose a private conference in the vestry. I am far from being sure that I might not have astonished our small congregation by resorting to this extreme measure, but for its being Christmas Day and no Sunday.

Mr Wopsle, the clerk at church, was to dine with us; and Mr Hubble the wheelwright and Mrs Hubble; and Uncle Pumblechook (Joe's uncle, But Mrs Joe appropriated him), who was a well-to-do corn-chandler in the nearest town, and drove his own chaise-cart. The dinner hour was half-past one. When Joe and I got home, we found the table laid, and Mrs Joe dressed, and the dinner dressing, and the front door unlocked (it never was, at any other time) for the company to enter by, and everything most splendid. And still, not a word of the robbery.

I opened the door to the company-making believe that it was a habit of ours to open that door-and I opened it first to Mr Wopsle, next to Mr and Mrs Hubble, and last of all to Uncle Pumblechook. N. B. *I* was not allowed to call him uncle, under the severest penalties.

'Mrs Joe,' said Uncle Pumblechook: a large hard-breathing middle-aged slow man, with a mouth like a fish, dull staring eyes, and sandy hair standing upright on his head, so that he looked as if he had just been all but choked, and had that moment come to; 'I have brought you, as the compliments of the season – I have brought you, Mum, a bottle

Mr Pumblechook's house, Rochester. (Geoff Doel)

of sherry-wine – and I have brought you, Mum, a bottle of port wine.'

Every Christmas Day he presented himself, as a profound novelty, with exactly the same words, and carrying the two bottles like dumb-bells. Every Christmas Day, Mrs Joe replied, as she now replied, 'Oh Un-cle Pum-ble-chook! This is kind! Every Christmas Day, he retorted, as he now retorted, 'It's no more than your merits. And now are you all bobbish, and how's Sixpennorth of halfpence?' meaning me.

We dined on these occasions in the kitchen, and adjourned, for the nuts and oranges and apples, to the parlour; which was a change very like Joe's change from his working clothes to his Sunday dress...

Among this good company I should have felt myself, even if I hadn't robbed the pantry, in a false position. Not because I was squeezed into an acute angle of the table-cloth, with the table in my chest, and the Pumblechookian elbow in my eye, nor because I was not allowed to speak (I didn't want to speak), nor because I was regaled with the scaly tips of the drumsticks of the fowls, and with those obscure corners of pork of which the pig, when living, had had the least reason to be vain. No; I should not have minded that, if they would only have left me alone. But they wouldn't leave me alone. They seemed to think the opportunity lost, if they failed to point the conversation at me, every now and then, and stick the point into me. I might have been an unfortunate little bull in a Spanish arena, I got so smartingly touched up by these moral goads.

Joe's station and influence were something feebler (if possible) when there was company, than when there was none. But he always aided and comforted me when he could, in some way of his own, and he always did so at dinner-time by giving me gravy, if there were any. There being plenty of gravy to-day, Joe spooned into my plate, at this point, about half a pint.

Have a little brandy, uncle, said my sister.

O Heavens, it had come at last! He would find it was weak, he would say it was weak, and I was lost! I held tight

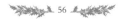

to the leg of the table under the cloth, with both hands, and awaited my fate.

My sister went for the stone bottle, came back with the stone bottle, and poured his brandy out: no one else taking any. The wretched man trifled with his glass – took it up, looked at it through the light, put it down - prolonged my misery. All this time, Mrs Joe and Joe were briskly clearing the table for pie and pudding.

I couldn't keep my eyes off him. Always holding tight by the leg of the table with my hands and feet, I saw the miserable creature finger his glass playfully, take it up, smile, throw his head back, and drink the brandy off. Instantly afterwards, the company were seized with unspeakable consternation, owing to his springing to his feet, turning round several times in an appalling spasmodic whooping-cough dance, and rushing out at the door; he then became visible through the window, violently plunging and expectorating, making the most hideous faces, and apparently out of his mind.

I held on tight, while Mrs Joe and Joe ran to him. I didn't know how I had done it, but I had no doubt I had murdered him somehow. In my dreadful situation, it was a relief when he was brought back, and, surveying the company all round as if they had disagreed with him, sank down into his chair with one significant gasp, 'Tar!'

I had filled up the bottle from the tar-water jug. I knew he would be worse by-and-by. I moved the table, like a Medium of the present day,' by the vigour of my unseen hold upon it.

'Tar!' cried my sister in amazement. 'Why, how ever could Tar come there?

But Uncle Pumblechook, who was omnipotent in that kitchen, wouldn't hear the word, wouldn't hear of the subject, imperiously waved it all away with his hand, and asked for hot gin-and-water. My sister, who had begun to be alarmingly meditative, had to employ herself actively in getting the gin, the hot water, the sugar, and the lemon-peel, and mixing them. For the time at least, I was saved. I still held on to the leg of the table, but clutched it now with the fervour of gratitude.

By degrees, I became calm enough to release my grasp, and partake of pudding. Mr Pumblechook had begun to beam under the genial influence of gin-and-water. I began to think I should get over the day, when my sister said to Joe, 'Clean plates - cold.'

I clutched the leg of the table again immediately, and pressed it to my bosom as if it had been the companion of my youth and friend of my soul. I foresaw what was coming, and I felt that this time I really was gone.

'You must taste,' said my sister, addressing the guests with her best grace, 'you must taste, to finish with, such a delightful and delicious present of Uncle Pumblechook's!'

Must they! Let them not hope to taste it!

'You must know,' said my sister, rising, 'it's a pie; a savoury pork pie.'

The company murmured their compliments. Uncle Pumblechook, sensible of having deserved well of his fellow-creatures, said – quite vivaciously, all things considered – 'Well, Mrs Joe, we'll do our best endeavours; let us have a cut at this same pie.'

My sister went out to get it. I heard her steps proceed to the pantry. I saw Mr Pumblechook balance his knife. I

saw re-awakening appetite in the Roman nostrils of Mr
Woplse. I heard Mr Hubble remark that 'a bit of savoury
pork pie would lay atop of anything you could mention,
and do no harm,' and I heard Joe say, 'You shall have some,
Pip.' I have never been absolutely certain whether I uttered
a shrill yell of terror, merely in spirit, or in the bodily hearing of the company. I felt that I could bear no more, and
that I must run away. I released the leg of the table, and ran
for my life.

But I ran no further than the house door, for there I ran
head foremost into a party of soldiers with their muskets:
one of whom held out a pair of handcuffs to me, saying,
'Here you are, look sharp, come on!'

The Twelfth Night Bride

In 1540, one of Henry VIII's men went over to Calais
in order to collect and to conduct the future Queen of
England, Anne of Cleves, a German and Protestant, to
her new royal home in England. Anne had been rec-
ommended to Henry as a successor to Jane Seymour
by Henry's 'spin doctor' Thomas Cromwell, and on
the strength of some flattering portraiture by Hans
Holbein. On New Year's Eve, Henry, who was lodged
at the Crown Inn at Rochester, decided to have a peep
incognito at his intended bride, and arrived together
with eight gentlemen of his Privy Chamber 'all dressed

Dover Castle.

alike in coats of marble colour.' Here things began to
go sadly wrong. Sir Antony Browne, who brought Anne
a New Year's gift, was struck with consternation when
he met the Queen-to-be, and later wrote that 'he was
never so dismayed in his life as to see a lady so far unlike
what was represented' (i.e. in her portrait). The King also
'recoiled in bitter disappointment,' and described her as
'a Flanders mare.' Another courtier, Lord Russell said
'That he never saw his Royal Highness so marvellously
astonished and abashed as on that occasion.' Anne on her
part was not particularly thrilled 'at the great, bloated
being who was to be her lord and master.' Though the
King privately grumbled, in public he received her
most graciously. Nevertheless, when he returned to
Greenwich he was in a foul mood and began to devise
schemes by which he could get out of his engagement.

Nothing could be done, for there was a political treaty as well as a betrothal contract to consider. Although Henry went through with the marriage ceremony, the marriage was never consummated as Henry claimed he was 'struck to the heart' and 'left her as good a maid as I found her.' Henry took out his spite against Cromwell and the fall of his erstwhile great friend and loyal servant can be directly attributable to the part he had taken in arranging this marriage. He was later executed. Eventually an annulment was arranged and Anne fully cooperated, which was fortunate as by this time Henry was already infatuated by one of Anne's ladies-in-waiting, Catherine Howard. Anne was rewarded for her compliance by being given a large income and several properties, including Hever Castle, the former home of Anne Boleyn.

The following account of Anne of Cleves' arrival and marriage in England was recorded by the Spanish Ambassador, Eustace Chapuys, in 1539 and 1540.

1539

This year on St. John's Day, 27 December, Lady Anne, daughter of the duke of Cleves in Germany, landed at Dover at 5 o'clock at night, and there was honourably received by the duke of Suffolk, and other great lords, and so lodged in the castle [the new Walmer Castle]. And on the following Monday she rode to Canterbury where she was honourably received by the archbishop of Canterbury, and other great men [Cranmer, five bishops, and the local clergy and gentry] and lodged at the king's palace at St. Austin's, and

Hever Castle. (Geoff Doel).

there highly feasted. Another source tells us that it was very foul weather when Anne arrived at Canterbury. She was received by torchlight with a great peal of bells, and was presented by Cromwell with fifty 'sufferans' [sovereigns] to which the City of Canterbury added fifty angels. On Tuesday she came to Sittngbourne (and Ospringe where she slept at the Maison Dieu).

1540

On New Year's Eve the duke of Norfolk with other knights and the barns of the exchequer received her grace on the heath , two miles beyond Rochester [Barham Heath] and so brought her to the abbey of Rochester where she stayed a that night and all New Year's Day.

And on New Year's Day in the afternoon the king's grace with five of his privy chamber, being disguised with

mottled cloaks with hoods so that they should not be rec-
ognised, came secretly to Rochester, and so went up into
the chamber where the said Lady Anne was looking out of
a window to see the bull baiting which was going on in
the courtyard, and suddenly he embraced and kissed her,
and showed her a token which the king had sent her for
New Year's gift, and she being abashed and not knowing
who it was thanked him, and so he spoke with her. But she
regarded him little, but always looked out of the window…
and when the king saw that she took so little notice of his
coming he went into another chamber and took off his
cloak and came in again in a coat of purple velvet. And
when the lords and knights saw his grace they did him
reverence…and then her grace humbled herself lowly to
the king's majesty and his grace saluted her again, and they
talked together, and afterwards he took her by the hand
and led her to another chamber where their graces amused
themselves that night and on Friday until the afternoon.

So she came to Greenwich that night, and was received
as queen. And the next day, being Sunday, the king's grace
kept a great court at Greenwich, where his grace with the
queen offered at mass, richly dressed. And on Twelfth Night,
which was Tuesday, the king's majesty was married to the
said queen Anne solemnly, in her closet at Greenwich, and
his grace and she went publicly in procession that day, she
having a rich coronet of [precious] stone and pearly set
with rosemary on her hair, and a gown of rich cloth of
silver, richly hung with [precious] stones and pearly, with
all her ladies and gentlewomen following her, which was a
goodly sight to behold.

The Anti-Methodists

Today, Methodism is so entrenched into the English religious scene that one may easily forget how its advent in the eighteenth century produced an explosive and aggressive response in some quarters. There was a varying response in Kent but attacks against the movement were particularly virulent in Canterbury, as can be seen from this description of an assault made against the person of a lay preacher and of the damage done to the fabric of his temporary meeting place – a house which he had hired in the Canterbury precincts. The *Kentish Post* for December 1750 indicates that a well-organised group of anti-Methodist activists had infiltrated the meetings on more than one occasion and had successfully caused damage and consternation, and also that the presumed same group of men had quite illegally broken into the preacher's house and had smashed up furniture. There being no police force at that time, the minister had called in soldiers stationed in Canterbury to stop the lawlessness. One really interesting point is that the editor of the *Kentish Post* reveals his bias by following the article with an advertisement for a recently published book written by an Anglican priest which condemns Methodism in quite blatant terms. From the *Kentish Post*, December 1750:

> Mr. Perronet, a Methodist, some time ago hired a house
> in Canterbury precincts where he preached to his breth-

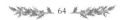

Old print of St Augustine's Gate, Canterbury.

ren; on Thursday some people interrupted him; on Friday
when he preached again they carried the pulpit outside
and burnt it with some forms; on Sunday they broke into
the house and broke a fine organ &c before being stopped
by a party of soldiers; Mr P had since removed from the
house.

The advert which follows:

*The Imposter Detected, or the Counterfeit Saint turned Inside
Out* by J Kirkby, rector of Blackmanstone, 'containing a full
discovery of the horrid blasphemies and impieties, taught
by those diabolical seducers called Methodists...particu-
larly intended for the use of the City of Canterbury, where
that mystery of iniquity has lately begun to work.'
(The book) to be had from the author, The Rev. Kirkby, or
Mr. Flackton, bookseller, one shilling.

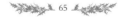

Ding Dong Battle of the Bells

The Church has used bells since its early days to summon the faithful to prayer and to mark the great festivals and they are particularly noticeable over the Christmas period. Those who give their services to their parish churches as bell ringers are justifiably proud of their efforts and usually well appreciated by their communities. The following is a cryptic resume of the accounts taken from the late November and December entries in the *Kentish Post* dated 1750, and tells the story of an epic battle between a set of church bell-ringers of Wye and some bell ringers in Dover. The enmity was sparked off when a Dover bell-ringer attended a service in Wye, found the performance wanting and wrote in to the local paper, the *Kentish Post*, claiming that the Wye performance was 'all fake and erroneous.' The bell-ringers of Wye were deeply offended and retaliated in print.

Resume of 'The Battle of the Bells' from the *Kentish Post*, 1750, from *Kentish Sources* Maidstone KCC, 1969:

The peal of grandsire triples rung by the gentlemen ringers of Wye said to be 'all fake and erroneous'.

Reply from Wye denigrating abilities of Dover ringer and challenging them to ring at Wye, with return at Dover, for eight to forty guineas; or at Wingham or North Romney; both sides to appoint a judge who will then

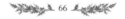

Early print of bell-ringers.

nominate a third. Wye accepts challenge to ring at Dover
and Wye; some Wye company to meet some of Dover at
an agreed place to stake money and settle Articles and
days of ringing; the grand peal with 194 bobs and forty
six singles completely rung on 30 November in 3 hours
31 minutes at the second time of trying 'although you
[i.e. Dover] thought we could never do it.' Five thousand
and forty quod and triples were rung at Wye by William
Drayner, Richard Dane, Daniel Fagg, Robert Baker,
Robert White, Thmas Tabraham, Thomas Waters, Thomas
Jarman.

Christmas Day in the Workhouse

There are elderly people living today who were born or spent some time as an inmate in a Kent workhouse. For most, there was a stigma attached to this, for although many could and did sympathise, society's erroneous perception of the inmates was often that the extreme poverty which had occasioned their entry was probably richly deserved. Families that were taken into a workhouse were often upset and demoralised by the fact that men and women were segregated within the workhouse set-up and the children, except for tiny babies, were removed from their mothers. Treats were few and far between, even in the twentieth century, and the joys of Christmas with its emphasis on family get-togethers and good will must have given the day an added poignancy.

Christmas Day in a workhouse in the early nineteenth century was always a day of rest but rarely more than that. When Victoria came to the throne in 1837 she inherited from the Poor Law Commissioners a ruling that nothing special in the way of a Christmas dinner should be served to the inmates. In 1840, the ruling was relaxed to allow 'extras' provided that they did not come out of union funds. This encouraged many philanthropists from local communities to come forward and to provide Christmas 'treats' for everyone in the way of foodstuffs. Albert's marriage to Victoria was particularly influential in changing the way in which the

The old workhouse, Headcorn, taken from the *Illustrated London News,* 18 August 1888.

English celebrated Christmas. The Germanic Christmas which Albert enthusiastically celebrated with his new royal family involved the Christmas tree (called a new-fangled 'novelty' by Dickens) magically lit up with candles and hanging with baubles, and the gifting of presents. The publication of Dickens' *A Christmas Carol* also helped create the idea of Christmas as a time of loving togetherness and charity towards the poor. By 1847, the new Poor Board Law (replacing the Poor Law Commissioners) graciously permitted a Christmas

dinner and additional 'extras' to be provided off the rates
in all workhouses.

The following is a pre-Christmas inspection of the
St John's Hill Workhouse, Sevenoaks, on behalf of the
Poor Board Law made in 1841; it is followed by descrip-
tions of Christmas dinners in some Kentish workhouses:

Bed-rooms, Boys – there are four allotted to the boys; the
largest measures 27 feet by 16, and 9 feet high. The next in
size, which opens into this, measures 21 feet by 16: there
are three windows in the first and two in the second,
and each of these rooms open at their further ends into
two very confined rooms. Which are used as workshops,
the one for tailors, the other for shoemakers from among
the boys. These rooms are very defective, not only from
the converging nature of the ceiling in the roof, but also
utterly inadequate to accommodate the present numbers
of inmates, which amounts to 62 boys and 2 men. This
number occupies 17 beds, 15 of which are six feet long by
four feet and-a-half, in each of which sleep four boys; in the
two others, which are about half the size, a man and a boy
sleep. There is only a space of about 13 inches between each
bed, the two flanking beds being pushed up close to the
wall, and a free passage down the middle of four feet wide.
The floors and walls were clean, excepting at one end in
each room, where the wall as well as the floor was soaked,
from a tub being kept in each room as a common recepta-
cle, instead of urinals for each bed; this is removed during
the day, but must necessarily be very offensive during the
night. The bedsteads were of iron, the bedding fairly clean

but old, especially the blankets, which were very thin, no under blankets being provided. The two other bed-rooms for the boys are at some distance from the above; they are both eight feet square and seven feet one inch high. Each of these small apartments contains two beds, which completely fill them; six children sleeping in each room; there was a window and door to each.

Bed-rooms, Girls – There are two bed-rooms for the girls; the larger open immediately out of their school-room, and measures 33 feet by 18; it contains nine beds, in which sleep 34 girls, besides a female attendant: the other is of the same size. Opening out of the former; it contains 10 beds with 40 children; the bedsteads are the same as the boys, but the beds and bedding are decidedly better. Both of these rooms are airy and spacious apartments, being well lighted and ventilated, with flat ceilings, and were very clean, a proper supply of urinals being provided.

Women and young children – Another room of the same size, for women and the younger children, contains nine beds, in four of which two women and one child sleep in each; in three others 12 children; and in the others, which are smaller, two children; this room was also clean and airy.

Bed-rooms, Women – There are two bed-rooms for the women, which are clean, airy, and spacious, with iron bedsteads and good bedding; in one of them they sleep two in a bed; in the other, which contains 10 beds, one child mostly sleeps in each.

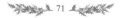

Bed-rooms, Men – There are three bed-rooms for the men; two of these measure 30 feet by 18, one being nine feet high, the other seven feet high; each contains 11 beds and 21 persons; a third room of the same size contains 10 and 20 persons; these rooms are equally well ventilated, airy and clean

The Lying-In Ward – Measures 12 feet by 10; we do not consider it well adapted for the purpose either in size or accommodation; it was warm when we visited it, and so far comfortable, but is deficient in a supply of water and the ordinary furniture requisite for such an apartment. It contains two beds, in which three persons at present sleep; viz., a woman lately confined with her infant in one, and the nurse with another woman, expecting shortly to be confined, in the other. On questioning her who had been recently delivered, she informed us that the sheets of her bed had been changed three times within the fort night, her body linen as often, and that she and her child had been supplied by the mistress with two dozen napkins, which were washed as often as necessary; this we consider sufficient. She likewise informed us that the fire is kept up during the day, and also all night if necessary; the bedding was excellent and the women looked healthy. Adjoining the lying-in ward is a small sleeping room without a fireplace, measuring nine feet and a-half by seven feet and a-half ; it contains two beds , in which at present sleeps the laundress, who acts occasionally as midwife in the absence of the medical man; the other is another woman expecting her confinement.

Cleansing Wards – We visited the two rooms called 'The Cleansing Wards', which are for the reception of paupers who have not been examined by the medical man, or undergone the usual cleansing before being allowed to mix with other inmates; they consist of a day and night ward for the men and the same for the women. The day ward for the latter being used for the bath-room. These rooms were 14 feet square; there was a good fire in each day-ward; each sleeping ward contained three beds, which were very old and dirty; there were two men on one side and two women and a baby on the other.

Daily Washing – The means for the daily washing in the morning are very defective, consisting merely of open sinks, exposed to the weather, instead of proper troughs in a room adapted for the purpose, and with a good supply of warm water, soap, towels &c. The half-cellar, halfout-house, which is occasionally used for this purpose is quite objectionable.

Sick-Wards – There are two, one for the males and one for the females; the former contained nine beds, of which all were occupied; the latter seven beds, of which five were occupied; the men's ward struck us as being close; these rooms measured 36 feet by 12, and were sufficiently lighted; they each had a water-closet attached.

School-rooms and Day-rooms – The school-rooms of the boys and girls, as well as also the day rooms for the men and women were airy and comfortable.

General Appearance of the Children – The general appearance of the children was remarkably healthy; there was not a single child in the sick wards.

Christmas in West Ashford Workhouse, 1915
From the *Tuesday Express*, dated 28 December, 1915

The inmates of West Ashford Workhouse had a very happy Christmas. On Christmas Day there was a service at 9.30a.m. conducted by the chaplain [The Rev. H. Boys Roberte]. Later, Mr. D. H. Headley [one of the Guardians] and friends gave gramophone entertainments to the infirmary inmates, and the Rev. A. H. Harrison [another Guardian] presented tobacco and tea and sugar to the inmates. The dinner consisted of roast beef, roast pork and vegetables, and the time honoured plum pudding with beer and minerals…and the officers of the institution assisted in making the poor people happy. At the close of a happy day the National Anthem was sung.

From the same paper and date:

At Milton Poor Law Institution the inmates spent an enjoyable day, winding up with Christmas entertainment which occupied the whole of the evening.

Christmas Day at Watts Almshouse

Dickens' heart-warming story *A Christmas Carol* is justly famous for its depiction of loving families happily celebrating Christmas round the hearth. As a writer, Dickens was to celebrate the ideal of the 'family' even though in his own youth, the late Regency period, Charles might well have been described as coming from a dysfunctional family. In particular, Charles had experienced real trauma when his improvident father had landed up in a London prison for debt and the young Dickens had been pulled out of school and sent to work long hours in a factory. The experience scarred him for life, for during this period of his father's imprisonment, the young Dickens was to experience poverty and shame and to suffer low self esteem. He had previously innocently considered himself as 'a little gentleman'; now he perceived his impoverished family as an object of shame and derision and in later life described the whole episode as a 'damnable Shadow which this father of mine (even now) casts upon my face'. One positive result of this miserable experience was that Dickens became acutely sensitive to the poor and their plight, and as a writer did what he could to jog the consciences of his reading public vis à vis the poor, and to remind them that at the coldest time of year they should be thinking of those less well off than themselves. This can be seen in this extract from 'The Seven Poor Travellers', written in 1854

Watts Charity Building, Rochester, 2002. (Geoff Doel)

Candidates for Watts Poor Travellers, 1881.

as a Christmas number for publication that year. It is one of his so-called 'frame' stories in which he introduces six fictional tellers of tales (seven if we include Dickens as the narrator) congregating in an ancient alms' house (Watts Charity) in 'the ancient little city of Rochester in Kent…on the twenty fourth of December.' Dickens was at that time rich and famous and living only a mile or so from Rochester at Gad's Hill, a substantial property with attached lands.

It being Christmas Eve, Dickens, as narrator, is 'possessed by the desire to treat the Poor Travellers [who have not yet arrived] to a Christmas supper' and a 'temperate glass of hot Wassail' (a hot Christmas drink consisting of beer, sugar, nutmeg and apples). The matron of the establishment obligingly gives her permission to the charitably-minded narrator who arranges with the local hotel to have a traditional Victorian Christmas dinner, with all the trimmings and finishing with hot plum pudding and mince pies, sent to the Watts Charity house that evening:

> I went back to my inn, to give the necessary directions for the Turkey and Roast Beef, and, during the remainder of the day, could settle nothing for thinking of the Poor Travellers. When the wind blew hard against the windows – it was a cold day – and dark gusts of sleet alternating with periods of wild brightness, as if the year were dying fitfully – I pictured them advancing towards their resting- place along various cold roads and felt delighted to think how little they foresaw the supper that awaited them. I painted their portraits in my mind, and indulged in little heighten- ing touches. I made them footsore, I made them weary; I made them carry packs and bundles; I made them stop by finger posts and milestones, leaning on their bent sticks, and looking wistfully at what was written there; I made them lose their way, and filled their five wits with appre- hensions of lying out all night, and being frozen to death. I took up my hat and went out, climbed to the top of the Old Castle, and looked over the windy hills that sloped down to the Medway; almost believing that I could descry some of my Travellers in the distance. After it fell dark, and the Cathedral bell was heard in the invisible steeple – quite a bower of frosty rime when I had last seen it – striking five, six seven; I became so full of my Travellers that I could

eat no dinner, and felt constrained to watch them still, in the red coals of my fire. They were all arrived by this time, I thought, had got their tickets, and were gone in – There, my pleasure was dashed by the reflection that probably some Travellers had come too late, and were shut out…

After the Cathedral bell had struck eight, I could smell a delicious savour of Turkey and Roast Beef rising to the window of my adjoining bed-room, which looked down into the inn yard, just where the lights of the kitchen reddened to a massive fragment of the Castle Wall. It was high time to make the Wassail…and I set out for Watt's Charity…

All [the] arrangements were executed in the most exact and punctual manner. I never saw a finer turkey, finer beef, or greater prodigality of sauce and gravy; and my Travellers did wonderful justice to everything set before them. It made my heart rejoice to observe how their wind-and-frost hardened faces, softened in the clatter of plates and knives and forks, and mellowed in the fire and supper heat while their hats and caps, and wrappers, hanging up; a few small bundles on the ground in a corner; and in another corner, three or for old walking sticks worn down at the end to a mere fringe; linked this snug interior with the bleak outside in a golden chain.

The Christmas story ends on Christmas morning and 'scarce daylight', with the narrator returning to the bosom of his family, having performed one last charitable deed – breakfast in the form of hot coffee and piles of bread and butter sent to the Travellers in the Watt's

Charity, for they are not permitted more than one night's lodging:

> While it was scarcely daylight, we all came out into the street together, and there shook hands.

From 'Pea Nut Corner'

AUNT AGATHA'S LETTER TO LITTLE ONES

The *Courier* newspaper throughout the war years ran a Pea Nut (Children's) Corner article which addressed itself to the child and was apparently very popular and probably influential. This Christmastime letter written in 1939 shows us Britain on the very threshold of world war and preparing for the unknown. Aunt Agatha is the very embodiment of the wise and sympathetic female aunt of the period – positive and pious – but there is understandably an anxious tone to the piece.

Dear Boys and Girls,

Here we are, in the first of December and Christmas will soon be here.

Of course it won't be like any other Christmases you have known before. This year there will be many strange, new things to try and make it difficult to have a merry Christmas. We have been asked not to be extravagant, and

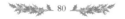

to help our country by wise and careful spending But we also want to remember the shop-keeper, whose trade is going to be badly hurt by a war-time Christmas, and so we can feel that whatever we do decide to spend will be helping him.

We won't be able to have the same great pile of parcels or the same exciting things to eat. But there's one thing we can have just the same, and that is our own Christmas thought of goodwill and love and the happiness of giving.

I hope I don't hear anyone say: 'Oh well, we can't give any presents this year. It's war-time.' Because that's just the wrong way to face Christmas 1939. Why can't you plan your presents and your happy thoughts exactly the same as other years? They won't be such expensive gifts, but you know how often we have said that it is never the size or the price of the gift that matters: It's the thought that is packed up inside. The tiniest, most inexpensive thing, something you may have made for somebody as you have sat by the fire on dark nights thinking of them on and off while you are busy with the making; some little gift you have bought for a few pence, perhaps it's only a Christmas card- these are the things out true friends cherish and Christmas wouldn't be so happy if our little remembrance were missing from among their parcels and cards.

So do let us try especially hard this year to carry out our Christmas plans with still more enthusiasm because it's war-time. You know how tremendously important it is to be continually sending out the right sort of thoughts these dark, sad days in which we find ourselves. And I know of no finer, easier way of thinking the highest and best and loveliest of peace thoughts – the kind that will help the Angels to overcome the powers of darkness- than those which spring straight from our hearts when we plan our little gifts and surprises for our dear ones and our friends at Christmas. There is no room for selfishness or greed or jealousy of any of the small, petty things that dog our minds and work on the side of evil. When we are thinking solely of giving somebody else happiness, then our minds are emptied of self and the good and beautiful streams of unselfish thought can flood them and create light.

If you can have a party, do have it, however humble it may be. Bring others into the circle of your happiness and share it if it's any way possible. Try to build for peace this Christmas by shedding as much of your own small light about you as you can. Try to carry on. That is the difficult but all-important task we each set this grey December, 1939. We will not lose our Christmas. We will plan for it just the same and draw as many others into it as we can. I rather feel our war-time Christmas will prove to be something very near to the heart of God.

> Yours affectionately,
> Aunt Agatha.

From The Twelfth Night Party, 1875
BY EVA KNATCHBULL HUGESSEN

Few journals written by children during the Victorian period have survived; and this account of a Twelfth Night children's party is a particularly interesting example. Eva Knatchbull Hugesson came from a distinguished Kent family and this account was written when she was eleven. Fifteen local children (all presumably of good family) had been invited to the party which was held in the family's very large house in Smeeth. We hear of the children being accommodated in the schoolroom where the girls and the boys (before being sent off to public school) were educated by tutors and governesses, and also a drawing room where the 'German Tree' decorated with candles had been set up surrounded by presents. The party is extremely well organised by the adults, with cousin Edith – presumably an unmarried relative – helping to supervise the event. Christmas crackers were invented in the 1840s by Tom Smith, a London confectioner, who included in his crackers sweets, paper hats and mottoes and these are very much enjoyed by the children. The party games finish with Snap Dragon, which was regularly played during the Twelve Days of Christmas. This involved a large meat dish full of raisins being set on a table. Children (and adults supervising) sat round about and someone set the dish alight by pouring on brandy and igniting it with a Lucifer. The dish flamed and the raisins jumped into the air while those round attempted to catch the fruit in their mouths without using their hands.

From the Diary of Eva Knatchbull Hugesson, 1873-75
Entry for 9 January 1875:

> Smeeth. In the afternoon we had our Christmas tree, we have been preparing it for days. Grandpapa, Cousin Edith, Howard and Mr. Donaldson were staying in the house. The children came at four. Two Perrys, four Bloomfields, five Robertsons, three Fords and a cousin of theirs came. First we played 'old soldier' and 'Hunt the slipper' in the schoolroom. Then cousin Edith came to tell us that the tree was lighted and we all went into the drawing room. The tree looked very well. Arthur and Ned cut the things

A Victorian children's party.

Victorian Christmas tree.

off, and shouted the numbers, I had some very nice things, among others, a large box of preserved fruit, two boxes of chocolate creams, and a little sort of cardboard house which opened at the top and had some plaster doll's food in it. After the tree, came tea in the dining room. Didn't the children stuff!!! Violet Perry had more than four pieces of cake! While they were all pulling crackers, eating sweets and reading mottoes, Ned and Donaldson prepared a dwarf together, Ned made the hands, Donaldson had a fright- ful mask on, which frightened some of the little ones and made them cry, but most of them laughed and liked it very much. Then we had a kind of dance in the drawing room, after which came 'Snap dragon!' Then a general wrapping up of toys, and they all went away!!!

From the *Kent County Examiner & Ashford Chronicle*, Christmas 1895

Our Ladies' Column

The 1880s which led into the 'naughty '90s' was an exceptional time for women generally. Young women of the middle classes could now enter centres of higher education (though not necessarily take degrees or other qualifications) and many became as well educated as their male counterparts. Much in vogue was the fashionable type-writing classes which were on offer – taking a qualification in this subject permitted young women who would normally have been forced to become governesses to work as secretaries and to join a work force which excitingly included men. The *Kent County Examiner & Ashford Chronicle* for this year is very daring in that it has employed a female journalist – obviously to attract a female readership – though they severely restrict her articles to subjects which today would be considered sexist – cooking, make-up, dress sense etc. They are further anxious to advise their female readers that their journalist is a 'lady' i.e. not of the working classes nor of lower middle classes, but of a class like their own. The Christmas article is therefore directed to ladies who have large establishments and give Christmas dinner parties, who employ cooks and servants and go by coach or horse-drawn cab to the pantomime. We have not tried out the pudding ourselves but are aware that it should be boiled in a large copper boiler in a traditional wash-house and that one's cook or servant should be in charge of the proceedings. Happy eating!

Specially written by a lady for the journal:

Now it is Christmastime, that season of good will and many presents, pudding and pantomimes, country house dances and town house dinners, a season when each takes his fellow by the hand (as I wish I could you, my readers) and wishes men 'a happy Christmas'. For the information of our lady readers we give the best recipe we know of for that Christmas plum pudding:

A Christmas Plum Pudding

Take three quarters of a pound of flour, two large tea-spoonfuls of Borwick 's Baking Powder, two ounces of bread crumbs, one and a half pounds of suet, two pounds of raisins, one pound of currants, ten ounces of sugar, two ounces of almonds, one pound of mixed candied peel, salt and spice to taste. Mix the ingredients well together and add six eggs, well beaten and three quarters of a point of milk, divide in two, and boil eight hours.

Boiling the Christmas plum pudding.

'Evacuese' or Enriching the English Language, Christmas 1940

Many Kent families were pressed into taking evacuees from London and elsewhere during the war years. The experience was not always a happy one, either for the Kent family or the evacuees involved, for the children were often unsettled, homesick and anxious for those who had been left behind. Sometimes, as in this case, taken from the *Courier* in 1940, the experience was actually an enriching one, and mutually enjoyable. Mr H.S.W. recognises gipsy words because he is a Man of Kent (or perhaps Kentish Man) with an interest in words and who has obviously met travellers working in the hop fields in the season. His Cockney evacuee uses gipsy words, not because he is a gipsy, but because he probably comes from a long line of East Enders who come down annually to Kent to pick hops and mix with the traveller workforce in the hop-gardens:

> My wife and I have an evacuee – a red-headed lad, with the physique of a buck-navvy, in spite of his recently achieved 16 years, a cheerful disposition, and a line in Cockney lingo that is a constant source of wonder and bewilderment to us.
>
> We call it 'evacuese' and treasure up any few gems of description that drop carelessly from his lips. If you were to ask us to 'come and have a butcher's' or politely pointed out to us that we had 'dropped our turts' we should know

exactly what you meant and be properly appreciative. But it got us groggy for a start.

The first time we have an inkling of etymological wonders in store for us was when our evacuee, who has a distinct way with the ladies, announced that he'd had a letter 'from a creamy.' We tried to look understanding. 'Creamy,' my wife said uncertainly. 'How delightful for you! Er, see now, what would a creamy be?'

Returning our look of puzzlement with one of astonishment he remarked tolerantly, 'You know. Creamy, creamy whirl, girl.'

And then we began to get the drift of the thing. So the next time he asked us what we thought of his 'pork' we thought hard and triumphantly arrived at the correct declension of pork – pork pie – tie and were appropriately approving about his choice in neck-wear which would certainly have dazzled cohorts of creamies.

'Plates of meat' for feet and 'pot and pan' for man were pretty easy, but this business of a 'turt' got us down. After we had struggled manfully to solve its hidden meaning we had to give up and have it explained to us that 'turt' was short for 'turtle-dove' which as all but the ignorant knew, stood for glove. We felt very humble after that, all the more so when we had to be told that quite obviously 'butcher's' stood for 'Butcher's hook' and thus with almost startling clarity, 'look.'

We learnt that 'stop rabbiting' would produce instant silence in our evacuee (well, fairly instantaneous) since 'rabbit and pork' stands for 'talk' and to be told to 'stop rabbiting' means 'shut up' in the vernacular of the provincials.

Things got a trifle complicated when we found that he mixed his 'evacuese' with what I always imagined to be gipsy words. When he said that it 'looked like parney' I know what he meant for once, but felt pretty sure it was the Romany word for rain. Similarly when he flashed a gold signet ring, enshrining a diamond amidst its wondrous scrolls, and asked whether we didn't think it was a nice 'piece of groyne' it was fairly obvious that he meant a piece of jewellery, but we have a shrewd suspicion that the word belongs to the Romanies and not to the Cockneys.

We occasionally startle him by inventing a Cockneyism ourselves, and as a party game this Christmas it has great possibilities. You might, for example, tell a player that you admired his 'whistle' and give him three guesses that it stands for 'whistle and flute' – 'suit.' Or there could be a competition to see who can make up most in a given time.

The thing has immense financial possibilities and I think I shall have to take out patents. Or write a dictionary.

H.S.W.

From *My Father as I Recall Him*
BY MAMIE DICKENS

Dickens bought Gad's House near Rochester in 1855 and lived there until his death in 1870. This is his merry record of December and Christmas in 1860 spent with his family of ten children; the season was an excep-

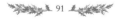

tionally cold one; it may be a reminder to many of pre-central heating days when even in every domestic house a coal-burning fireplace was required to heat the bedrooms and an 'en-suite' consisted of a water jug and pitcher and 'potty' kept in a cupboard or under a bed.

> 1860 – in our warm dining-room on Christmas Day, we could hardly sit at the table. In my study on that morning, long after a great fire of coal and wood had been lighted the thermometer was I don't know where below freezing. The bath froze, and all the pipes froze, and remained a stony state for five or six weeks. The water in the bedroom jugs froze, and blew up the crockery. The snow on the top of the house froze, and was imperfectly removed with axes. My beard froze as I walked about, and I couldn't detach my cravat and coat from it until I was thawed at the fire.

Mamie Dickens' recollections of how her father spent Christmas at Gad's Hill: From *My Father as I Recall Him*, (Roxburghe Press, 1897):

> Christmas was always a time which in our home was looked forward to with eagerness and delight, and to my father it was a time dearer than any other part of the year. He loved Christmas for its deep significance as well as for its hoys, and this he demonstrates in every allusion in his writings to the great festival, a day which he considered should be fragrant with the love that we should bear one to another and with the love and reverence of his Saviour and Master. Even in his most merry conceits of Christmas,

there are always subtle and tender touches which will bring tears to the eyes, and make even the thoughtless have some special veneration for this most blessed anniversary.

In our childish days my father used to take us, every twenty-fourth day of December, to a toy shop in Holborn, where we were allowed to select our Christmas present, and also any that we wished to give to our little companions. Although I believe we were often or more in the shop before our several tastes were satisfied, he never showed the least impatience, was always interested, and as desirous as we, that we should choose exactly what we liked best.

When we were only babies, my father determined that we should be taught to dance, so that as early the Genoa days we were given our first lessons. 'Our oldest boy and his sisters are to be waited upon next week by a professor of the noble art of dancing,' he wrote to a friend at this time. And again, in writing to my mother, he says: 'I hope the dancing lessons will be a success. Don't fail to let me know.'

When the 'boys' came home for the holidays there were constant rehearsals for the Christmas and New Year's parties; and more especially for the dance on Twelfth Night, the anniversary of my brother's Charlie's birthday. Just before one of these celebrations my father insisted that my sister Katie and I should teach the polka step to Mr Leech and himself. My father was as much in earnest about learning to take that wonderful step correctly, as though there were nothing of greater importance in the world. Often he would practise gravely in a corner, without either partner or music, and I remember one cold winter's night his awakening with the feat that he had forgotten the step so strong upon him

Gad's Hill interior with Christmas tree, December 1996. (Geoff Doel)

that, jumping out of bed, by the scant illumination of the old-fashioned rushlight, and to his own whistling, he diligently rehearsed its 'one, two, three, one, two, three' until he was once more secure in his knowledge…

But I think that our Christmas and New Year's tides at Gad's Hill were the happiest of all. My father himself always deserted work for the week, and that was almost our greatest treat. He was the fun and life of those gatherings, the true Christmas spirit of sweetness and hospitality filling his large and generous heart. Long walks with him were daily treats to be remembered. Games passed our evenings merrily. 'Proverbs', a game of memory, was very popular, and it was one in which either my aunt or myself was apt to prove winner. Father's annoyance at our failure sometimes was very amusing, but quite genuine. 'Dumb Crambo' was another favourite, and one in which my father's great imitative ability showed finely. I remember one evening his dumb showing of the word 'frog' was so extremely laughable that the memory of it convulsed Marcus Stone, the clever artist, when he tried some time later to imitate it.

Our Christmas Day dinners at Gad's Hill were particularly bright and cheery, some of our nearest neighbours joining our home party. The Christmas plum pudding had its own special dish of coloured 'repousse' china, ornamented with holly. The pudding was placed on this with a sprig of real holly in the centre lighted, and in this state placed in front of my father, its arrival being always the signal for applause. A prettily decorated table was his special pleasure, and from my earliest girlhood the care of this devolved upon me.

He was a wonderfully neat and rapid carver, and I am happy to say taught me some of his skill in this. I used to help him in our home parties at Gad's Hill by carving at a side table, returning to my seat opposite him as soon as my duty was ended. On Christmas Day we all had our glasses filled, and then my father, raising his, would say, 'Here's to us all, God bless us!', a toast which was rapidly and willingly drunk. His conversation as may be imagined, was often extremely humorous, and I have seen the servants, who were waiting at table, convulsed often with laughter at his droll remarks and stories. Now, as I recall these gatherings, my sight grow blurred with the tears that rise to my eyes. But I love to remember them, and to see, if only in memory, my father at his own table, surrounded by his own family and friends – a beautiful Christmas spirit.

Ghostly Apparitions at Christmastime in Kent

Kent has its fair share of ghouls and ghosties. There are coaches without visible drivers racing at great speed along lonely Kent roads at dead of night; pale phantoms endlessly perambulating along the wainscoted corridors of great Kentish houses and castles; there are horrid shrieks of heartless murderers resounding forever in a time-loop along with the sad plaints of unavenged victims – all vouched for by generations of Kentish witnesses. In this chapter we have made a list (hopefully comprehensive) only of those ghosts who make special spectral appearances on Christmas Eve or thereabouts. We make no claims regarding the veracity of the following list of seasonal apparitions in Kent…but there are those who would.

The ancient town of Rochester in east Kent is dominated by a massive keep built in the reign of Henry I. Close-by stands the great twelfth-century cathedral and clustering around it the remains of some of its former monastic buildings, the ruined chapter house and the cloisters. Three ancient gates, Priors Gate, Deanery Gate and Chertsey's Gate give entrance into the High Street. The last gate appears as Jasper's Gate in Charles Dickens' last and unfinished work, *The Mystery of Edwin Drood*.

Nearby is the Corn Exchange, from the front of which projects a huge clock on an ornamental bracket

which became the 'moon faced clock' of Dickens' *The Uncommercial Traveller*. It is before this clock on Christmas Eve that the spectre of Charles Dickens, evidently reluctant to leave his beloved Kent in which he spent the happiest days of his life, is said to appear. At the last stroke of twelve, Dickens slowly takes a gold watch from out of his waistcoat pocket… and solemnly checks the time before dematerialising in the early morning air.

The south coast of Kent had a unique sighting of a ghost ship at Christmastime. The story began 100 years ago when a cross-Channel paddle steamer named the SS *Violet* was driven onto the Goodwin Sands during a violent winter snowstorm. The wintry seas were mountainous and all hands and passengers drowned. At the start of the Second World War, a man on duty on the East Goodwin lightship reported an old-fashioned paddle steamer in difficulties on the sands. The lifeboat raced out to investigate… but there was nothing to be seen, only snow-capped waves.

The picturesque North Downs village of Kemsing on the Pilgrim's Way resounds to the sound of a horse's hooves every Christmas Eve when the spectre of a Norman Knight, bent on the murder of Becket, primate of all England, rides up to the ancient church and dismounts before the door.

Hever Castle in west Kent, the beautiful one-time home of the wealthy American Astor family, can boast a royal ghost, Anne Boleyn, the second in Henry VIII's line of unfortunate wives. Hever was once the home of the Boleyn family and Anne's ghost is said to manifest

The 'moon faced clock',
Rochester High Street.
(Geoff Doel)

itself each Christmas Eve when her spectre lingers for
a few moments on the bridge which spans the moat.
This lovely castle was owned by Anne's father, Thomas
Boleyn, and it was here that Henry first courted and,
some say, made her sister pregnant before turning his
amorous attentions to the unfortunate girl who would
for such a brief period become Queen of England and
mother to Queen Elizabeth I.

Rainham in north Kent would have us believe that a
phantom coach makes a regular spectral Christmas Eve
appearance. This coach, driven by headless coachman,
pulled by headless horses and with a headless passen-
ger inside, is said to leave the church at a rapid pace
and, with only one very brief (and apparently needless)
stop to water the headless horses, races to Bloor's Place

Hever Castle.

where it turns into the grounds and promptly melts into the early-morning air. Until relatively recently, a glass of brandy was left out for the refreshment of the phantom traveller.

The superstitious will avoid a Christmas Eve visit to the Mourning Tree – a Canadian cypress growing in the churchyard of Bearstead village. Sited a little way along the Ashford Road out of Maidstone, for generations it was surrounded by cherry orchards and hop fields. This tree was planted by the vicar who mark the grave of a nineteen-year-old boy, John Dyke, who had been publicly hanged on Penden Heath on Christmas Eve 1830, accused of firing a hayrick. Tragically only a few years after the hanging a local man made a deathbed confession to the crime. When his body was interred, the coffin was deliberately set on the other side of the churchyard 'so that his presence shall not offend the innocent spirit of the scapegoat.'

When Thomas à Becket was brutally murdered in Canterbury Cathedral on the fourth day of Christmas, his body was laid on a bier before the high altar and his brains and blood collected and preserved separately. Drops of this blood were later enclosed in tiny lead flasks which were sold as pilgrims' badges and which were reputed to have healing powers. The contents of the flasks was known as 'Canterbury Water'. In Canterbury itself, the sainthood of the murdered prelate was soon made manifest to the citizens by the fact that the public well in Sun Street ran red with the saint's blood. A red and gold pump fixed high up a wall today marks the

The Dark Entry, Canterbury.

original site of the miraculous well. Thomas never reappeared as a ghost but the beautiful medieval windows in Canterbury portray him occasionally flying in and out of his gold and gem encrusted shrine in full bishop's regalia in order to perform miracles.

One last ghost will always appear in Canterbury the Friday before Christmas Day (or indeed on Christmas Day itself if it falls on Friday), because she makes a spectral appearance every single Friday in the year without fail. Her name is Nell Dunn and her story is set in Canterbury in 'bluff King Harry's days' prior to the Reformation. She was by all accounts a very pretty and substantial young woman and served as cook and mistress to one of the Cathedral canons. This lecherous and faithless canon introduced a younger and prettier mistress into his house whom he pretended was his 'niece.' After six weeks, Nell could stand it no more and poisoned them both. Nell then abruptly disappeared – it was rumoured that she was buried alive under the heavy paving slabs of the Dark Passage, possibly by the other canons. From this spooky spot Nell emerges to haunt the area every Friday night, including Christmas week. The Revd Richard Barham (1788-1845), who wrote under the pseudonym Thomas Ingoldsby, included her story in his collection of Kentish legends, *The Ingoldsby Legends*. These stories, in verse and prose, appeared periodically in *Bentley's Miscellany* in 1837, a magazine edited by Dickens and with illustrations by Tenniel, Leech and Cruikshank. One slight problem is that no one knows if he made the story up or if it is a genuine Kent legend.

Christmas in the Kent and Sussex Hospital, 1943

We have included this piece because it is an apt reminder of how hard the staff worked in our Kent hospitals during the Second World War and how unstinting they were with their time and talents – and also how appreciative the patients were.

From the *Courier*, 1943:

A real Christmas atmosphere pervaded the Kent and Sussex Hospital. Gaily decorated wards, smiling countenances and plenty of all those good things which make for a happy time at this season of the year turned the whole hospital into a 'dream home' where no one was overlooked. Always quite a notable feature were those wards which sparkled with all kinds of decorative art so effectively arranged by members of the nursing staff, and giant Christmas trees ladened with suitable gifts added to the brightness. On Christmas Eve there was carol singing in all the wards to herald in the great occasion and then on the morning all the patients were delighted to greet the Mayor [Alderman C.E. Westbrook] who made his usual tour with a cheery word for all the patients.

Those who looked forward to all the luxuries associated with Christmas dinner were not disappointed. Even if there were many homes without turkey, it was not so with the Hospital. Those responsible for the catering arrange-

Malcolm Ward as Father Christmas in the Westerham Mummers Play at the Fox Inn, January 2009. (Geoff Doel)

ments had managed to lay in store sufficient to meet the needs, consequently everyone who was fit enough to enjoy 'given the bird' was provided with this delicacy and other good things to go with it. If there was a difference in the Christmas pudding it was not so much the ingredients which were good and plentiful but the spirit that flames when the pudding is brought in. Sparklers were used instead. That was the only difference. A generous public had seen to it that Apples were also plentiful.

Members of the honorary and resident staff did the carving and waited on the patients, and Mr. Jarvis made an admirable Father Christmas. In the afternoon there was a concert by the nursing staff which was repeated on Monday.

Probably the happiest of spirits were to be found in the Children's Ward. Here again the patients woke to find the ward a veritable fairy land with a big Christmas Tree, decorated with all kinds of gifts which are treasured by the young folk. Father Christmas had also left a 'bag' of toys at all the beds.

Staff members and sisters had their Christmas dinner at a time when they were able to enjoy it. Altogether it was a very happy occasion for everyone.

A grateful patient writes to the Editor: 'I have in other years read your article on Christmas at the Kent and Sussex Hospital, and have been very interested in them. This year, I am an in-patient in hospital, and wish to tell your readers of the splendidly happy time which we had. On Thursday evening a mixed choir snag beautifully in all the corridors, for which we all thank them. A procession of our nurses, sister and doctors carrying lanterns sang carols round the wards – a most impressive sight which I shall always remember. Then came Christmas Day with the visit of the Mayor and friends; the lovely dinner – turkey carved in the wards by the doctors, whom we patients would like to thank for untiring devotion and determination that we should have a happy time. The festivities concluded on Monday afternoon with a super concert by the nurses which was thoroughly enjoyed. I for one will never be sorry for anyone who has to spend Christmas in hospital.'

A Christmas Hunt, 1902

The West Kent Hounds hunted the district round Sevenoaks, Tonbridge and Wrotham; the area was divided by a large tract of unhunted country from East Kent; the Ashford and Headcorn district was hunted by the Mid-Kent Stag-hounds.

The following is a record of the Christmas hunt by the Master of the East Kent Hounds for Wednesday 12 December 1902 from his hunting diary. In all, eight hunting days were recorded in the diary over the Christmas period. Among the New Year hunts a large field met at Elvington Court and 'two good runs were enjoyed, one of an hour and fifteen minutes, and the other of fifty minutes, each ending with a kill'. The final hunt on 8 January records that the 'fox was pulled down handsomely close to Wootton, after a run of an hour and fifty minutes':

Hounds met at Smeeth station. After drawing Backhouse blank, a move was made for the Aldington Woods, where we were not long before we heard view-holloa on the Knoll, and as we went to it information was conveyed by signal and otherwise that a fox had gone away. I learned he had a good five minutes' start. Hounds were desperate eager to get on but held together till we rounded the hill, where they felt for, and soon picked up the scent. They went off with a good cry, and at a fair pace. Some of knowing ones

The hunt.

on the ride were inclined to hustle hounds before they had properly settled down and established a scent. The line was over a nicely fenced country that required a little doing, and some of the fences took toll of one or two impetuous spirits, which steadied the field, a bit. After fifteen glorious minutes we were all on good terms with the pack, and the best with each other and our horses, and I was able to see which hounds were cutting out the work. Two officers from Shorncliffe and two farmers were prominent in front, and close on our wake thundered and crashed a score or more of the field.

The pace was kept for another twenty minutes over large grass enclosures. There was no perceptible change in scent,

The East Kent hounds, 1814.

and hounds were soon pointing towards the Stouting Hills, rising in front of us and they got on the base of them. We could hear hounds chiming merrily as we felt we might have to take more out of our horses than they had to give. I watched the pack swing up the slope. Will the fox sink the wind, or will he keep on up wind? He chose the latter. We lost sight of the pack for a few minutes, and I was beginning to feel anxious, when some sheep in the distance wheeled round and gave us an inkling of the direction hounds had gone. We were now in the hill country, with large coverts in the distance; fences were few, but once on the top of the hill, good going. Hounds checked above Stouting village but cast themselves forward, hitting him off just as we got up to them, and I cheered them on. Hounds running was hard as ever, entered Stouton Rough, and on to West Wood, to Sibton Wood. Here we had some very pretty hunting;

A running fox.

hounds were desperately keen and unmistakably near their fox, but scent was not so good, and one after another would carry it for a short while then fall back and allow a slower hunter to take it on, and follow the short turns the fox was making. It was an anxious time as they almost walked after their fox on to the public road, where hounds checked, but old Tomboy hit him off up the Wood, and proclaimed his find with a deep-toned roar. Never was a note more welcome and never did huntsman tingle more. The hounds dashed to their old comrade, took the line steadily on to the Plantation and Elham Park and the covert, where the fox lay down. Old Sailor, Sepoy and Rattler ran mute with their hackles up as they crashed through the broom, the fox a few yards ahead of them. Hounds, getting a view, opened their throats, and threw their tongues with all their might, as they hurled themselves at him, and pulled him down in the open as he wheeled round to face them! 'Whoo-oo-oo-oop! old lads, tear him, and eat him up!' from half a dozen throats. 'Well done, old lads; ten, twelve, fifteen, seventeen couple, only one hound short!' A seven-mile point, over vale, hill and wood. Here comes the Secretary, must try him for a drink, as he generally carries a big flask. My throat was like a lime-kiln. Once more, 'Whoo-oo-oop!'

Christmas for Troops Away From Home, Sittingbourne, 1915

At the start of the First World War in 1914, England was caught up in a patriotic fervour. It was firmly believed that war would only last a year and that the vast numbers of older boys and young men who had volunteered were heroically 'doing their bit' and that should they fall in battle, their sacrifice would be noble. December 1915 began to mark a different mood in Britain. The Army and Navy were now caught up in great theatres of war throughout Europe, the Near East and India. In early December 1915, troops were gradually being withdrawn from Gallipoli and many of the wounded mentioned in the extract may have served in campaigns there. Gallipoli had proved a disaster but few knew as yet that it was due to bad planning and leadership as well as shortage of ammunition and inadequate equipment. As we know now, there were other great battles soon to be fought, including the Somme, the second battle of Ypres and Passchendale to mention but three, all with terrible slaughter on either side and with the men enduring the most appalling hardships. This tiny extract is poignant in that the men are spending a wet Christmas away from home, with only cigarettes, a good meal and a film-show to cheer them up before being sent to the front. The *Tuesday Express* reported on 28 December 1915 that:

Barges carrying the wounded from the Dardanelles to hospital ships.

Christmas Day, in spite of wet weather, was spent in happy fashion by the troops at Sittingbourne. Christmas fare of a sumptuous character was provided for dinner, followed by smokes, ad lib. In the evening, the Queen's Picture Hall had been secured, and the soldiers were entertained to a first class picture and variety show, which was after their own heart, and which was highly appreciated. At the Glover's and Whitehall Hospitals the wounded soldiers were royally entertained at Christmas dinner, and the rest of the day was devoted to social enjoyment and variety entertainments.

The Procession of the Boy Bishop

Kent is fortunate to have numbers of surviving references to dramatic spectacles and ritual drama and its performances in the Middle Ages. There were, for example, street processions of the Boy Bishop during the midwinter period, a popular custom dating from the late twelfth century and centring around the election of a 'Boy Bishop' from amongst young church choristers. The custom is known to have taken place in Rochester and Canterbury Cathedral Schools, as well as in the collegiate church and a number of other parish churches in Kent. including New Romney; the latter appropriately dedicated to St Nicholas, the patron saint of children and our proto-Santa Claus. The election was probably held on 6 December (St Nicholas' Day) and was the prelude to a week-long series of activities known as the 'Feast of Boys'. The mini-bishop was dressed in full bishop's attire along with a mini mitre and crozier, all expensive items. After vespers on St John's Day (27 December) the boy bishop led a singing procession of choristers to the High Altar, the latter dressed as the 'higher' clergy in silk copes and carrying candles. They were followed by the adult chapter. The boys then seated themselves in the stalls in the choir which were normally used by the men and their little 'Bishop', presumably in the most important seat, 'officiated' at all the services except mass. Ronald Hutton, in his book *The Stations of the Sun,* claims that it was usual during this festival to have

The Boy Bishop.

a candlelit street procession of the little choristers, who sang as they processed, during which 'the little prelate' blessed the spectators and collected money from them for parish funds'. A surviving reference to the New Romney 'Boy Bishop Procession' indicates that New Romney Church took its procession to nearby Lydd. The custom was banned by Henry VIII in 1541.

Christmas Greetings from Folkestone Post Office, 1917

The collection, dispatch and delivery of mail has always been an important part of the work of the Post Office, particularly at Christmastime. In this extract the First World War is in its third year and we see that women are now engaged in the war effort and are doing men's work at home, including the delivery of mail and parcels.

From the *Kentish Express & Ashford News*, 29 December 1917:

> During the Christmas 'pressure period' Folkestone P.O. dealt with 200,000 'outward' letters and packets, while the 'outward' parcels numbered between 5,000 and 6,000 a day. The 'inward' mail from the Army Post Office (Normally about 10,000 a day) rose to 20,000 a day, while parcels coming into the district averages 5,000 or 6,000 a day. The general delivery of letters and packets in the Folkestone

A postman.

district for the week represented a grand total of 185,000. On Christmas Eve, the Mayor (Sir Stephen Penfold) visited the PO and conveyed Christmas greetings to the staff paying in the course of his remarks, a graceful tribute to the admirable work of the women now engaged in the Post Office Service.

Christmas at Maidstone Prison

From the diary of a Prison Governor at Maidstone Prison at the end of the nineteenth century, we learn that Christmas was not permitted to be celebrated by the inmates; neither was there a Christmas dinner. The Governor, however, instigated a party for the children of his warders in 1882 and commemorated the event with this brief entry in his diary:

> 28 December, 1882 Holy Innocents' Day. Entertained the warders' children [33] to tea, games, supper, Christmas Tree, toyes [sic], etc and 6d each.

Nearly fifty years would pass before prison inmates in Maidstone could expect to celebrate Christmas. This happened when Major B.D. Grew, who had entered the prison service in 1923 after a background in the Army and whose extensive prison work experiences had been obtained in Borstal, Rochester Prison and Wormwood

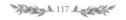

Left: A prison warden.

Below: Maidstone Prison.

Scrubs, took over the governorship of Maidstone Gaol and implemented new ideas and 'experimental reforms.' His notes for 1931 tells us that there were about 300 inmates at the time, figures that included reprieved murderers (the death penalty was still extant) , the 'usual crop of housebreakers and thieves' and a 'large number of sex offenders including homosexuals' (homosexuality was still a crime at this period and one which carried a stiff prison sentence). Major Grew permitted the men to celebrate Christmas in their cells, to put up decorations and receive and send Christmas cards, and had them served a traditional Christmas dinner with all the trimmings. A decorated tree was also set up in the prison for all to enjoy.

Save Fuel This Yule

We love the emotive martial language with which a military Commander now in charge of a desk job in the Ministry of Fuel and Power addresses the civilian population (mainly housewives) as if they were conscripts newly arrived at the Front.

From the *Herne Bay Press*, 19 December 1942:

Commander Stephen Kinghall, MP, of the Ministry of Fuel and Power, sends this to the civilian front: –

'Your Country Needs You'.

Going over the top is always a critical moment, and we have reached it in the Battle for Fuel. Why do I say this? With Christmas the real winter starts and we are entering those grim months from January to March that will test us to the full as soldiers in this vital struggle on the Home Front.

The enemy is moving up his reserves. The icy fingers of winter are stretching out to try to paralyse our transport system – the line of communication that brings the coal to our homes, or to the gas works and electric power stations. We must not wait for that to happen. We must attack and so make sure that, whatever apparent success the foe may have, he will not penetrate our defences. The Order is – Stiffen your resolution and put slack on your fires.

Frugal but Festive: 'For Father – Christmas Day Pudding' Wartime Style

This recipe was sent out to wartime Britain by the Ministry of Food, London W1, and appeared in the *Herne Bay Press*, 26 December 1942, just a little late in the day for Christmas Day itself:

Rub 3 ounces of cooking fat into 6 tablespoons of flour until like fine crumbs. Mix in 1½ breakfast cupfuls of stale breadcrumbs, 1 lb pruned (soaked 24 hours, stoned, chopped) or any other dry fruits such as sultanas, 3 oz sugar, 1 teaspoonful mixed spice, ½ teaspoonful pf grated nutmeg. Then chop 1 large apple finely, grate one large raw carrot and 1 large raw potato, add to dry ingredients. Stir in three reconstituted dried eggs. Mix one teaspoonful of bicarbonate of soda in 1 tablespoonful of mixed lemon substitute and stir thoroughly into the pudding mixture. Put into 1 large or 2 small well-greased basins, cover with margarine papers and steam 2½ hours. This can be prepared overnight and eaten on Christmas Day.

Fogbound Evacuees Sheltered at Tonbridge, 1944

From the *Sevenoaks Westerham Courier and Kentish Advertiser*, Friday 22 December 1944:

Throughout the week Tonbridge children who were evacuated to the West Country at the commencement of the 'flying bomb' attacks have been returning to their homes under the Government scheme. Approximately five hundred children have come back, the first train load being welcomed at the station by members and officials of the Urban Council including the Chairman (Councillor H. W. Christie) and the Vice-Chairman (Councillor L. Hearmon), the Clerk (Mrs S. J. Thorne), the Chief Warden (Capt. J.C. Woodward), the A.R.P. Officer (Mr. F. Bristow)

and the W.V.S. Centre Organiser (Miss F. M. Fayerman).
On the eve of Wednesday week, the worst 'pea souper' of
the season caused the train carrying the evacuees returning to other parts of Kent and Sussex to be delayed several
hours, and early in the evening notice was sent to the local
authorities to have food and shelter ready for about twenty
five children. The Rest Centre at the Congregational
Church was thrown open and on their arrival about 8
p.m. The evacuees were served with hot soup, sandwiches
and tea. The beds were put up in the two halls, but as the
evening wore on and still more weary travellers arrived the

Tonbridge Castle. (Geoff Doel)

vestry also had to be commandeered. By eleven thirty pm there were nearly one hundred children and thirty adults at the centre. Beds were everywhere and two of the guides had to sleep in the Church itself.

Spirits, however, did not flag, and one nine year old boy entertained his companions by reciting long humorous poems. Not a grumble was heard from anyone, although willing helpers got home at about 2 a.m.

Breakfast was served at 8 a.m. the next morning and by midday the evacuees had all departed by bus, train or car.

From *Black's Guide to Kent*, 1866

The beautiful ruins of the old castle at Scotney, a moated manor, is now maintained by the National Trust. It takes its name from its first owner, Lambert de Scoteni, who came over with William the Conqueror. The following extract deals with Scotney in the last years of Elizabeth I, a turbulent time not unlike our own, when religious differences meant that certain families, because of their religious persuasion, were perceived as being linked with terrorism, treachery and conspiracy. The families were accordingly kept under surveillance with occasional 'raids' on their property. This account details one such raid on Scotney, and 'a great escape.' Any priest caught who was known to have performed the sacraments was liable to be hung, drawn and quartered after brutal interrogation. The Darrells, who were sheltering Father Blount, could also have been imprisoned and tortured – and could also have been put to death.

From *Black's Guide to Kent*, 1866:

Scotney was ever the home of romance, for one of its earliest owners, Walter de Scotney, was executed at Winchester in 1259 for administering poison to the Earl of Gloucester and others. The humour of it is that Walter de Scotney was probably quite innocent. The Earl recovered, but his brother, William de Clare died, as also did the Abbot of Westminster. The Earl himself seems to have had a narrow escape, for he lost hair, nails, teeth, and skin, and must have been one vast comprehensive ache, and in a more painful condition that that of a chicken plucked alive.

Scotney Castle.

Scotney then passed to the Darrells, who led a finely dramatic life here until they ended, to an effective and tragical 'curtain.'

The old castle lies in a watery hollow beneath the modern Gothic mansion, and itself consists of two distinct portions: the castellated building erected about 1418 by Archbishop Chicheley, and the later manor-house of the Darrells, who, in Queen Elizabeth's time were Roman Catholics, maintaining their religion and its observances in spite of laws, ordinances, and penalties levelled against Papist recusants.

To secure their officiating priests against arrest the Darrells contrived a highly ingenious hiding-hole in their mansion, and it was speedily found useful. It was the Christmas night of 1598, towards the end of Elizabeth's long reign, and Father Blount, a well-known and keenly sought priest, was in the house with his servant when the party were surprised by a search expedition, who, having got wind of Blount's presence, were bent on capturing him.

While the enemy were demanding admittance, Blount and his servant were hurried into the courtyard, where a huge stone in the wall, turning upon a pivot, gave entrance to the hiding-place. Unluckily for them, a portion of a girdle-strap was caught between the stone and the rest of the wall, and showed plainly. Meanwhile the search-party had been admitted, and, securing the inmates of the house in one room, proceeded to search the place.

While they were thus engaged an outside servant of the family changed to see the girdle, and promptly cut if off, calling as loudly as he dared to the fugitives to pull in the fragment that was still visible. The sharp-eared search-party, hearing a voice in the courtyard, rushed out and sounded the walls all round, without making any discovery, but kept it up until the rain, which had set in, disgusted them, when they retired, intending to resume the search on the morrow.

As Blount's own record of the adventure tells us, he and his servant were concealed for days under a staircase. At last afraid to risk the result of another day's proceedings, they escaped under cover of night. Barefooted they crossed the court-yard, climbing the walls and swam the moat, then covered with thin ice. They did well to fly, for next day their hiding place was discovered.

In later years the castle and manor-house, by that time ruined, was the haunt of smugglers, among whom the Darrells themselves were reputed to be prominent.

The Westerham Mummers Play of the Seven Champions

This text was kindly supplied by David Hicks of Ravensbourne Morris. It was noted down on 18 July 1953 by Jeff Metcalf, founder-member of Ravensbourne Morris Men and former Squire of the Morris Ring, from Mr J. Medhurst at the Bat and Ball Inn, Leigh, near Tonbridge. Mr Medhurst had moved to Leigh from Sundridge (3 or 4 miles from Westerham). He was aged 72 in 1953 and first took part in the play when he was about 16, i.e. 1896-97. It must have carried on into the twentieth century, but he was very vague about when it was last performed. It was an adult affair with no boys teams; Mr Medhurst said that he introduced the play to Sundridge from Westerham. He said that there were sometimes two or three teams of Champions in the area and that before Christmas, they went round the big houses in the usual manner.

Dress was old clothes with bits of coloured paper or rags sewn on – not too many. All the performers had black faces – other special features of dress are indicated below. Each man remained outside the door until it was his turn to speak: the instructions were to 'say it steady'.

Mummers plays are short, traditional, ritualistic plays generally performed over the Christmas period, featuring a Father Christmas, two boasting champions who fight, one being killed and - in a ritualistic sequence - revived by a mysterious well-travelled and socially superior Doctor. Various begging characters then ask for money – usually Johnny Jack ('wife and family on my back') and Beelzebub in the Kent versions. There seems to be a symbolic or sympathetic magic connection with the life-force and/or passing of the seasons at the midwinter period.

Mummers plays were common in rural areas in many parts of England; they are rare in eastern coastal regions and the east coast of Kent is no exception, preferring the Hooden Horse midwinter ritual, with the exception of a controversial play collected in Dover (for text see our *Mumming, Hoodening & Howling: Midwinter Rituals in Sussex, Kent & Surrey*, Meresborough Books). But seven more or less complete texts known as 'The Seven Champions' survive from west Kent villages and small towns, as well as text fragments and memories of many more. The earliest west Kent text collected, that from Shoreham as performed in the 1890s, is published in our *Folklore of Kent* (The History Press).

The Darent Valley was (and still is) a fruitful area for mummers plays, the Westerham Play (featured below) is documented as moving to Brasted and Sundridge in the late nineteenth century and the Brasted Champions are known to have performed at Toys Hill, Ide Hill, Westerham and Sundridge and included visits to several large houses before the First World War. The Ravensbourne Mummers currently perform the play regularly over the Christmas and New Year period. The Shoreham Champions visited pubs in Shoreham, Otford, Eynsford and Bat and Ball; their costumes were ribbons sewn onto old clothes.

The Medway Valley is another focal point for mumming plays. Regular traditional performance of the West Malling Mummers Play survived remarkably late – into the 1930s. Local interest has helped in the preservation of enough of the list of characters, text and costume details to enable a very lively revival of the tradition since the 1980s. It is still going strong, with a team organised by Alan Austen, a Malling folklorist, singer, musician and Morris dancer. The play is performed on the Saturday evening before Christmas, when most of the local hostelries are visited and about eight performances given.

Above: Photo of Brenchley Mummers, *c.* 1920. (Photo courtesy of *Roundabout* village magazine at Brenchley and Matfield)

Left: St George – the Westerham Mummers Play performed by the Ravensbourne Mummers at the Fox Inn, Keston, January 2009. (Geoff Doel)

Anthony Cronk in his *A Short History of West Malling* (1951) mentions the play:

> Then at Christmastide, there was the genuine West Malling folk-play, 'The Seven Champions', which was regularly performed by local stalwarts right up until 1930, the players travelling round the taverns and private houses in the same manner as carol singers…The actors wore outlandish costume, and all had blackened faces except St George, who wore a brass helmet with a plume resembling that of a life-guardsman.

The Honorary Secretary of the Rotary Club of Malling, Mr J.A. Dawson, wrote to Alan Austen about the play in 1982:

> I was able to recall the Mummers at West Malling…about 1912 or 1913. My memory is of about four players dressed in highly coloured military uniforms which probably came from the Boer War era. They would visit houses just before Christmas and have sham sword fights outside the front doors of houses with much worthy shouting conversation of which in my youthful eight years I could not understand a word.

The Bearsted Play is well documented, being referred to in Chamber's 'List of Texts' in *The English Folk Play* as being in a 'MS of Miss Coombes'. *A History of Bearsted and Thurnham* (1939) quotes a booklet dealing with village traditions, including the annual appearance of the Seven Champions in earlier days:

The Turkish Knight from the Westerham Mummers Play.

Another event was the appearance of the Seven Champions just before Christmas. They would appear dressed in paper to suit the part and recite such strains as 'I'm little Jack Sweep, all the money I get I keep' and 'Here I come, Beelzebub! In my hand I carry a club, in my hand a dripping pan, don't you think I'm a jolly man'. The words would be followed by the beating of the pan with the Club and we hope the money gained covered the depreciation of the utensils.

Recently, a photograph of what seems to be a double Mumming team (i.e. with characters duplicated) has come to light from Brenchley – from around 1920. This is the only archival Mummers photo we know of from Kent and we have included it in this book, courtesy of the *Brenchley and Matfield Magazine*:

The Christmas Champions or The Old Christmas Champions

FATHER CHRISTMAS: (in false beard and wig made from clothes line)
'In comes I, old Father Christmas.
Am I welcome or am I not?
I hope old Father Christmas will never be forgot.
For in this room there shall be shown
The greatest battle that ever was known.
Step in. King George with thy free heart.
To see if thou can'st claim peace for thine own heart.'

KING GEORGE: (wears a cardboard crown, and carries a wooden sword; tall)
'I am King George. That man of courage bold;
With my broadsword and spear I won ten crowns of gold;
And if any man dare enter this room
I will hack him small as dust,
Afterwards I will send him to the cookery shop
To be made into mince pie crust.'

TURKISH KNIGHT: (small man, carrying wooden sword)
'In comes I, little Turkish Knight.
In Turkish land I learned to fight.
I'll fight King George, that man of courage bold.
And if his blood be hot, I'll quickly make it cold.'

The Combat from the Westerham Mummers Play.

KING GEORGE:

'Ho, Ho, my little fellow, thy talk is very bold;

Just like one of these little Turkish knights that I have been told

Pull out your sword and fight;

Pull out your purse and pay;

For satisfaction I will have before I go away.'

TURKISH KNIGHT:

'Satisfaction – or no satisfaction;

For my body is lined with steel,

And therefore I'll fight any man.

With my broadsword and steel.'

(They fight, and during this the Old Woman (wearing skirt and bonnet) enters and stands behind the Turkish Knight.

The Turkish Knight has a small bag of ochre fixed to his chest, and when King George pricks this, the Turkish Knight falls back into the arms of the Old Woman. He does NOT fall to the ground).

OLD WOMAN:
'Oh, Oh. King George, what hast thou done?
Thou hast cut and slain my only son.
Is there a doctor can be found
To cure this man lying bleeding in my arms.'

ITALIAN DOCTOR: (top hat and frock coat)
'In comes I. an Italian Doctor
Just lately come from Spain.
I can cure the sick, and raise the dead again.
I have a little bottle in my waistcoat pocket.

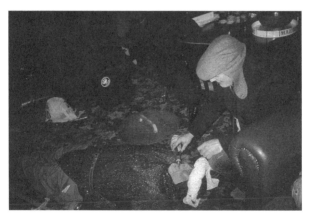

Revival of the slain champion.

It's called the golden frosty drop (produces small bottle)
If I pour a drop on his nose (does so)
And a drop on the roof of his tongue (does so)
And say to him - arise. go home. and tell your country
What an Italian Doctor has done for thee.'

(The Turkish Knight recovers and walks away)

JOHNNIE JACK: (should be the smallest man, and has sewn onto his jacket-back a piece of cardboard about 18 inches square, with 5 dolls – the biggest in the middle)

'In comes I. little Johnnie Jack,
With my wife and family on my back.
My family's large, but I am small,
But every little helps us all.'

ALL:
'A jug of brown ale makes us merry and sing;
Money in our pockets is a very fine thing.
Now ladies and gentlemen. Just at your case.
You may give us Christmas Champions just what you please.'

The performance finished with a little music. Popular tunes of the day played on mouthorgan, tambourine, triangle.

The First Wasseling Cuppe from A Perambulation of Kent, 1570

BY WILLIAM LAMBARDE

The term 'wassailing' derives from the Anglo-Saxon words *waes hail* (be healthy). A famous Kent legend, first recorded by Geoffrey of Monmouth in his *History of the Kings of Britain* (of around 1136) tells how Reinwin, daughter of the fifth-century Germanic leader Hengist, greets the British leader Vortigern, who falls in love with her and marries her, disinheriting his children and causing civil war, with a toast 'wassail' at a banquet. The story is repeated by later Kent writers such as William Lambarde in his *Perambulation of Kent* and in the Kent tradition the lady becomes known as Rowena. Although in Kent, with its prolific cider orchards, apple wassailing predominated, there was also a general midwinter/ Christmas custom of wassailing in which seasonal toasts of mulled wine, spiced ale or cider were drunk from a wassail bowl at feasts during house-to-house visitations by bands of wassailers, probably the originators of perambulatory carol singers. Surviving wassailing songs are not specifically religious, but invoke good health on visitants and visitors; a typical wassail song collected from neighbouring Sussex has the refrain:

And may joy come to you and to our wassail.

Origin of the Wassail Bowl, by James Godwin.

The favourite Kent telling of the story is in William Lambarde's *Perambulation of Kent* in 1570 under the title of 'Roxena – the first wasseling cuppe':

> Hengist espying therefore, that King Vortiger was muche delighted in woman's companie... he had him to a solemn banquet, and after that he had... well plied him with pots, he let slippe before him a faire gentle-woman, his owne daughter, called Roxena, or Rowen, which being instructed before hand how to behave herself, most amiablie presented him with a goblet of wine, saying in her owne language 'Hail, noble king, wassail Lord King' ... with which daliance, the King was so delighted, that he not only vouchsafed to pledge her, but desired also to perform it in the right manner of her owne countery. And therefore he answered (as he was taught unto her againe, drinc hael...

David Hicks of
Ravensbourne Morris takes
round the Wassail Bowl at
the Fox Inn, Keston, January
2009. (Geoff Doel)

Partaking of the Wassail
Bowl at the Fox Inn,
Keston, January 2009.
(Geoff Doel)

Which when she had done, himself tooke the cuppe, and pledged her so hartely, that from thenceforth he could never be in rest, until he had obtained her to wife, little weighing, either how deeply he had endaungered his conscience in matching himselfe with a Heathen woman, or how greatly he had hazarded his crowne by joyning handes with so mightie a foreign nation.

At the time of this marriage, Hengist (labouring by all meanes to bring in his owne countriemen) begged of the king the territories of Kent, Essex, Middlesex, and Suffolke, (then knowne by other names) pretending in worde, that he would, in consideration thereof, keep out Aurel. Ambrose (a competitor of the crowne) whose arrival King Vortiger had much feared'.

From *History and Topographical Survey of the County of Kent* 1797–1801
BY EDWARD HASTED

Apple wassailing is a custom from the cider producing counties of Kent, Sussex, Somerset, Devon and Herefordshire and is a good example of the rural tradition of sympathetic magic. A libation of cider punch was given to a representative cider apple tree in early January to invoke a bountiful crop of cider apples in the orchard the following Autumn. The earliest known reference

Firing at the apple trees.

to this custom comes from the county of Kent – from the village of Fordwich near Canterbury in 1595. Two centuries later, Edward Hasted describes the custom in his *History and Topographical Survey of the County of Kent* (1797-1801), though puzzlingly placing it during Rogation week:

> There is an odd custom used in these parts, about Keston and Wickham, in Rogation week; at which time a number of young men meet together with a most hideous noise, run into the orchards, and incircling each tree pronounce these words:
>
> > 'Stand fast root, bear well top;
> > God send us a YOULING sop!
> > E'ry twig, apple big;
> > E'ry bough, apple enow!'

For which incantation the confused rabble expect a gratuity in money, or drink, which is no less welcome. But if they are disappointed of both, they, with great solemnity anathematise the owners and trees, with altogether as insignificant a curse.

It seems highly probable that this custom has arisen from the antient one of perambulation among the heathens, when they made their prayers to the god, for the use and blessings of the fruits coming up, with thanksgivings for those of the preceding year. And as the heathen supplicated Eolus, god of the winds, for his favourable blasts; so in this custom, they still retain his name... this ceremony being called 'Youling', and the word is often used in their invocation.

Typically as a classicist of the period, Hasted invokes the classical wind-god, but 'Youling' is much more likely to be derived from the Anglo-Saxon and Scandinavian name of 'Yule' for the midwinter feast and this further confirms the midwinter, sympathetic magic and likely early origins of the custom.

The surviving words of the 'Blean Hoodening Song' sung around the parish of Blean, near Canterbury, on Christmas Eve, suggests a tradition of apple wassailing in East Kent as well, perhaps linked with the distinctive East Kent tradition of the Hooden Horse:

Three jolly hoodening boys
Lately come from town
Apples or for money

We search the country round;
Hats full, caps full,
Half bushel baskets full –
What you please to give us
Happy we shall be.
God bless every poor man
Who's got an apple tree.

We have not discovered any evidence for the custom surviving the First World War in Kent, but there have been a number of revivals, notably the Chanctonbury Morris Men wassailing the apple trees at Tenterden in the 1970s and the Tonbridge Mummers and Hoodeners

David Hicks of Ravensbourne Morris wassails the apple tree at the Fox Inn, Keston, January 2009. (Geoff Doel)

blessing the apple trees on New Year's Day at Cob Tree in the 1990s. Alan Austen organized a revival at Brogdale for a number of years and this year (January 2009) we were kindly invited to the Ravensbourne Morris Apple Wassailing at Keston, where a wassail bowl of cider is passed round, then poured as a libation to the tree (see photographs). The Westerham Mummers play was also performed and included a Hooden Horse surviving from the 1930s. A memorable evening.

From *The Hooden Horse*, 1909
BY PERCY MAYLAM

100 years ago a Canterbury solicitor, Percy Maylam, published his classic study of the Hooden Horse in a limited edition of 303 copies, with seven original photographs. This edition is rare and highly valuable. We have reproduced extracts in three books and this year Geoff has combined with Percy Maylam's great-nephew, Richard Maylam, and Mick Lynn to publish a centenary edition of Percy's book through the History Press with introductory essays and including Percy's other classic study on the Kent custom of Gavelkind.

Midwinter rituals of dressing up as horses and horned animals are widespread throughout the British Isles, and indeed throughout Europe. The East Kent tradition of 'hoodening', in which a man disguised himself as a horse by crouching under a sacking or hop pocket covering, holding a pole with a carved wooden horse's head attached to it, survived in the Isle of Thanet, Deal and Walmer into the early twentieth century and has been revived more extensively in Kent in the late twentieth century.

The horse was traditionally accompanied by a Waggoner, Jockey, Mollie (a man disguised as a woman with blackened face and with a besom broom) and musicians, though as the custom declined, the number of participants shrank also. In Thanet, the Hoodeners visited farms over the Christmas period; in Walmer and Deal they visited shops (open until 8 p.m. on Christmas Eve), pubs and hotel bars. Naomi Wiffen of Edenbridge wrote to us in the 1980s:

Hooders from Walmer Court Farm. Photographed at Walmer, 29 March 1907. (H.B. Collis). From Percy Maylam's *The Hooden Horse*.

I remember as a child being taken out on Christmas Eve
to the High Street in Deal where the shops would be open
very late, and it was the only time Deal children were
allowed out in the evening, as parents were very strict. As
we would be looking at the lighted shops, and listening
to the people selling their wares, a horrible growl, and a
long horse's face would appear, resting on our shoulder
and when one looked round, there would be a long row of
teeth snapping at us with its wooden jaws. It was frighten-
ing for a child. Usually, there would be a man leading the
horse, with a rope, and another covered over with sacks or
blankets as the horse.

Walmer Hooden Horse rearing. Photographed at Walmer, 29 March
1907. (H.B. Collis). From Percy Maylam's *The Hooden Horse*.

Walmer hoodeners holding the horse's head, with three bells (showing its place in the team of farm horses). Photographed at Walmer, 29 March 1907. (H.B. Collis). From Percy Maylam's *The Hooden Horse.*

Percy Maylam's book cites an account in the *Church Times* in 1891 about involvement in the custom in the 1840s:

When I was a lad, about 45 years since, it was always the custom on Christmas Eve with the male farm-servants from every farm in our parish of Hoath and neighbouring parishes of Herne and Chislet, to go round in the evening from house to house with the Hoodining Horse, which consisted of the imitation of a horse's head made of wood, life-size, fixed on a stick about the length of a broom handle; the lower jaw of the head was made to open with hinges, a hole was made through the roof of the mouth, then another through the forehead coming out by the throat, through this was passed a cord attached to the lower jaw, which when pulled by the cord at the throat caused it to close and open; on the lower jaw large-headed hob-nails were driven in to form the teeth. The strongest of the lads was selected for the horse; he stooped and made as long a back as he could, supporting himself with the stick carrying the head; then he was covered with a horse cloth, and one of his companions mounted his back. The horse had a bridle and reins. Then commenced the kicking, rearing, jumping, etc, and the banging together of the teeth. As soon as the doors were opened the 'horse' would pull his string incessantly, and the noise made can be better imagined than described. I confess that in my very young days I was horrified at the approach of the hoodining horse, but as I grew older I used to go round with them... There was no singing going on with the hoodining horse, and the party was strictly confined to the young men who went with the horses on the farms. I have seen some of the wooden heads carved out quite hollow in the throat part, and two holes bored through the forehead to form the eyes. The lad who played the horse would hold a lighted candle in the hollow, and you can imagine how horrible it was to one who opened the door to see such a thing close to his eyes.

Percy Maylam first encountered the Hooden Horse whilst spending Christmases with his uncle at Gore Street, Monkton from 1888-92:

Anyone who has spent a Christmas in a farm-house in Thanet - it has been my good fortune to spend five - will not forget Christmas Eve; when seated round the fire, one hears the banging of gates and tramping of feet on the gravel paths outside (or, if the weather be seasonable, the more cheerful crunching of crisp snow), and the sound of loud clapping. Everybody springs up saying, 'The hooden-ers have come, let us go and see the fun'. The front door is flung open, and there they all are outside, the 'Waggoner' cracking his whip and the leading the Horse (the man who plays this part is called the 'hoodener'), which assumes a most restive manner, champing his teeth, and rearing and plunging, and doing his best to unseat the 'Rider', who tries to mount him, while the 'Waggoner' shouts 'whoa'! and snatches at the bridle. 'Mollie' is there also! She is a lad dressed up in woman's clothes and vigorously sweeps the ground behind the horse with a birch broom.

There are generally two or three other performers besides, who play the concertina, tambourine or instruments of that kind. This performance goes on for some time, and such of the spectators as wish to do so, try to mount and ride the horse, but with poor success. All sorts of antics take place, Mollie has been known to stand on her head, exhibiting nothing more alarming in the way of lingerie than a pair of hobnail boots with the appropriate setting of corduroy trousers. Beer and largesse are dispensed and the performers go further. Singing of songs and carols is not usually a part of the performance and no set words are spoken. In Thanet, occasionally, but not always, the performers, or some of them, blacken their faces. Years ago, smock frocks were the regulation dress of the party.

In a house which possesses a large hall, the performers are often invited inside; at times the horse uses little ceremony, and opening the door, walks in uninvited'.

Feeling that the Hooden Horse was becoming an endangered species in the Edwardian period, Percy Maylam researched at first hand and photographed the Hoodeners of St Nicholas-at-Wade in 1905, Walmer in 1906 and Deal in 1907, as well as doing extensive newspaper archival research for his book. His accounts of the three teams are accurately observant as to both the details of the enactments and the Hooden Horses, and the sociological background; his book is a very enlightened piece of Edwardian folk research. Here is Percy Maylam's account of his visit to see the Walmer Hooden Horse:

Hoodening at Walmer. Shortly before Christmas, 1906, I had a conversation with Mr Vaughan Page, of Canterbury, as to the observance of the Custom at Walmer. He told me that his father (Mr Henry Page) recollected the custom at Walmer back to, at any rate, 1849, in which year he became tenant of Walmer Court Farm, remaining there until 1896. During this period the men on Walmer Court Farm always went round at Christmas with the hooden horse; the musicians who accompanied them relying to a large extent on sheep-bells – one in each hand. They had no Mollie.

Mr P. T. Greensted, who succeeded Mr Page, and was tenant of Walmer Court Farm until 1903, informs me the custom went on during the whole of his time. I subsequently ascertained that the leader at Walmer was Mr Robert Laming of May's Lane, Walmer.

On Christmas Eve, 1906, I went to Walmer, and having ascertained the time when the party would set out, I had a comfortable tea at the hotel near Walmer Station. While at tea, a man in grotesque attire came into the room, and proceeded to blacken his face with burnt cork at the fire. I, who had thoughts for nothing but hoodening, enquired if he were one of *that* party. 'No,' he said, and it appeared he was one of the Walmer Nigger Minstrels with no very great opinion of such obsolescent customs as hoodening.

However, very shortly afterwards, the well-known clap! clap! was heard from within the bar – the Hoodeners had come. I hastened to see them. The party consisted of four: the hoodener with the horse's head, the man whose duty it is to lead the horse, and when not doing so to play the triangle, and two musicians, one playing the tambourine

Hooden Horses and Mark Lawson at the Gate Inn, Marshside,
November 2000. (Geoff Doel).

and the other the concertina. The wooden head is made
on the same lines as the Thanet horse, but it is somewhat
larger and the jaws open much further back and therefore
wider. Here I found the practice was that the 'gratuity'
had to be placed in the horse's jaws, and on this particular
occasion the horse put his head on the counter of the bar
while the landlord's little daughter was lifted up from the
other side in order to carry out the proper form of giving
the money, after conquering her fright, real or feigned, she
accomplished her task. I had a short conversation with the
leader, Mr Robert Laming, he told me that his horse was
not the one which used to belong to the Walmer Court
men; he did not know what had become of that, that he
had been out with his horse on Christmas Eve for this five
and twenty years and missed doing so only one year. The

Walmer party were in their ordinary clothes, but formerly I was told, they wore smock frocks; they had no Mollie, nor any recollection of her. I accompanied the party a little way on their rounds which I was told would not finish till about eleven o' clock: it was then six-thirty, and I found the Hoodeners sure of their welcome, the horse gambolled into all the crowded shops, and at Christmas they are crowded, and every one was pleased except a collie dog which worked himself into a fearful age but feared to try his teeth against the wooden jaws of the horse. On visiting the butcher, he, regardless of the gramnivorous habits of the animal, placed a mutton chop in the jaws besides the accustomed tribute, a piece of humour which met with great applause.

Sadly Maylam's fears for the immediate future of the Hooden Horse were realised. In the short term his own interest helped to stimulate a revival of the St Nicholas-at-Wade tradition, including the reintroduction of the Mollie and besom broom for his photographs. However, the traditions ended soon after the First World War, though with revivals beginning from the late 1930s, and there are a number of teams once again today, and a number of original horses have been discovered.

From *Handbell Ringing & The Mistletoe Bough*
BY KEN THOMPSON

Handbell ringing is a distinct custom practised all year round in Kent and elsewhere, but handbell ringers were always particularly in demand at Christmas. Hop farmer and traditional singer Ken Thompson remembered his father handbell ringing on Christmas Eve 1923 at the family farm at Little Betsoms. Ken worked at Little Betsoms Farm near Westerham between the wars as a boy and in 1950 took over the farm tenancy from his father. Little Betsoms was principally a sheep farm on the North Downs, though some dairy cattle were kept and hay grown. Fran interviewed Ken and taped his reminiscences of handbell ringing:

From Westerham you climb up to the North Downs and at the summit the land levels out.

If you look to your left there's a pair of old slate cottages known as the Fort Cottages. The Fort Cottages were service cottages to the old Napoleonic fort behind, then pretty derelict and overgrown, and my father was employed as caretaker and gardener to the lodge at Westerham Heights. It was in No. 1 Fort Cottages that I was born and is the setting for my first childhood memories.

It was 1923 and the approach to Christmas and I was wakened by the sound of ringing bells. I climbed out of my

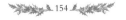

Ken Thompson, front left, picking hops into a bin on his Faversham farm in the 1950s.

cot and opened the door into the living room where, to my amazement, I saw a number of whiskery men standing all round the room. The fire was flowing and it reflected their ruddy tanned faces and brass bells shining in their hands.

'You should be in bed,' said my mother.

But she was very good and let me stay and watch the bell-ringers. I can see them now, their old faces shining. They'd obviously had a drink and were enjoying themselves. The oldest men seemed to have one bell in each hand, the others, two bells in each hand and then there was my father. I can remember even now the pride with which in later days he used to say, 'I had to play four in each hand'. When they turned their wrists the Christmas tunes rang out.

The bell-ringers visited each others' houses in turn and also went round to the big halls and houses. The object of

this was to raise money for their societies and of course they'd get a drink. That's how it went on then. I was hardly more than three or four at that time. It's amazing how clear the memories are.

I remember too that my mother always kept a pig which was killed just before Christmas. Some of it was sold and some of it kept for the family.

Fort Cottages were at the end of an old lane that ran back maybe three-quarters of a mile off the road and at the end of that lane was Little Betsoms Farm, about ninety-five acres plus woodland. When I was about five or six I was to move there with my parents when my father took over as tenant farmer. That takes me back to another childhood Christmas memory. It was 1926 and when we all woke up on Christmas morning there was more snow than I think anyone had ever seen in their lifetime. Of course we kept sheep up on the North Downs – Romney Marsh sheep that came up from the marsh for the winter to get away from the wets – and by Boxing Day all those sheep had been drifted in. Well, there was my Uncle Thew who was a gun-layer in the Navy, home for Christmas, and my brother Bill and my Father and they were all big chaps and out they went with their big coats on and their shovels and spades to see what they could do about finding the sheep. And about half past twelve in they came and they'd got all the sheep out. They'd dug about but the only way they could find the sheep was by spotting the number of little holes in the snow drifts made by the breathing of the sheep. When they'd found these air-holes they'd found the sheep. And they got them all home in the barn and put them in and made them comfortable and of course when these chaps came indoors they were more than pleased to have a drop of whisky and my mother was standing on the step waiting and so was I and they told us how they got out the sheep and they were really quite proud of what they'd done.

Now that snow went on and it got worse and it meant that farms like ours, high up on the North Downs, became isolated and food had to be dropped by bi-plane. I remember now walking with my brother to Westerham and walking right over the frozen drifts and over the hedges! You couldn't tell where the hedges were – the only things sticking out of the snow were tall trees and the tops of buildings. Of course the old church steeple in Westerham stood out like a landmark. And all the local men were out digging foot roads for none of the builders or anybody else for that matter could go to their work. It was a long time before the roads were clear but when they were I remember having to walk the two and a half miles to the bakers in Biggin Hill with a sledge and picking up six loaves at a time (great big double loaves) and dragging them back home.

Of course my mother used to talk to me about Christmas past but there wasn't much to tell because she came from a family of eighteen and their Christmases were pretty poverty stricken. She used to tell me that the only way they got any Christmas at all was by going out carol singing at the big houses in Tatsfield. They'd do a bit of singing and they used to come up with a few halfpence and that would be taken home to her mother (my grandmother) and then they were alright for a bit of Christmas pudding.

My mother told me that it was just a white pudding with a few currants so it wasn't the great big brown luscious affair that we have today.

Ken remembers his mother singing the gothic Christmas ballad of 'The Mistletoe Bough' (written by Thomas Bayly in the early nineteenth century) and it was also in his repertoire and sung by him at our Tonbridge Folk Club. The song concerns a bride trapped in an old chest whilst playing hide and seek. The Mistletoe Bough was a very popular Christmas ballad in the nineteenth and early twentieth centuries in virtually all the southern counties and is found extensively in the oral tradition and in written sources. Another Kent traditional singer, Les Waghorn, remembers hearing it sung between the wars in the Headcorn area and it is in the current repertoire of the Millen Family of Smarden. Thomas Hardy mentioned it in his novel *A Laodicean* and the Copper family of Rottingdean have a Sussex version.

These versions almost certainly derive from the ballad of the same name composed by the Gothic writer Thomas Bayly (1797-1839), set to music by Sir Henry Bishop. The original heroine of the tale is Ginevra of the Orsini family of Modena, who hid herself in a chest during a game on her wedding night, but in the folk-song this event has merged with English traditions concerning the Lovell family, the supposed chest being on show at Malmesbury Abbey:

The mistletoe hung from the Castle wall
The holly bough hung in the old oak hall
And the Baron's retainers were blithe and gay
All keeping their Christmas holiday.
The Baron beheld with a father's pride
His beautiful child, young Lovell's bride,
Whilst she with her bright eyes seemed to be
The star of that goodly company.

Chorus:
O the mistletoe bough
O the mistletoe bough

I'm tired of dancing my love', she cried,
'Here tarry a moment for me to hide.
And Lovell, be sure thou art first to trace
The clue to my secret hiding place.'
Away she ran and her friends began
Each tower to search and each vault to scan.
And young Lovell cried 'O where dost thou hide.
I long to find you my own dear bride.'

O the mistletoe bough.
O the mistletoe bough.

They searched all that night and they searched the next day,
They sought her in vain till a week passed away.
In the highest, the lowest, the loneliest spot,
Young Lovell sought wildly and found her not

And years flew by and their grief at last
Was told as a sorrowing tale of the past.
And when Lovell appeared, the children cried,
'See the old man weeps for his own dear bride.'

O the mistletoe bough.
O the mistletoe bough.

One day an old chest that had long lain hid
Was found in the castle, they raised the lid.
And a skeleton form lay mouldering there
In the bridal wreath of a lady fair.
O sad was her fate, in a yuletide jest,
She hid from her lord in the old oak chest.
It closed with a spring – what a dreadful doom
The bride lay clasped in a living tomb.

O the mistletoe bough.
O the mistletoe bough.

Edward IV's Christmas at Eltham Palace

In the Middle Ages, royalty and the aristocracy celebrated the Twelve Days of Christmas in festive style. *The Chronicles of Croyland* describes Edward IV's 1482 Christmas at Eltham Palace. The King was 'clad in a great variety of most costly garments, of quite different cut from those which had hitherto been seen in our country'. There were 2,000 guests and the food supplied for the Twelve Days of Christmas was as follows:

> 1,000 sheep, 2,000 swans, 6 bulls, 400 peacocks, 4,000 bitterns, 4,000 dishes of jelly, 1,000 cold venison pastries, 300 calves, 1,000 geese, 1,200 plovers, 200 cranes, 200 heronshaws, 2,000 hot custards, 15,000 hot venison pastries, 800 pigs, 2,000 capons, 2,400 quails, 2,000 kids, 1,000 curlews, 12 porpoises and seals and plenty of spices, sugared delicacies and wafers.

'Going Home', taken from 'Old Christmas Customs', the *Illustrated Sporting & Dramatic News*, 27 December 1884.

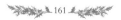

The Plum Pottage Riots at Canterbury

In the seventeenth century, Canterbury was a battleground for the very survival of the celebration of Christmas in the Civil War. Loyalties in Canterbury were closely divided between the Royalist and Parliamentarian causes and when the Puritan Mayor, William Bridge, proclaimed in December 1647 that by Order of Parliament 'Christmas Days and all other superstitious festivals are utterly abolished', there was trouble! The Mayor proclaimed that the usual Saturday market would be held on Christmas Day and that all shops should open and that no church services were to be held. He threatened prosecution or arrest for anyone who hung 'rosemary, holly, or bayes or other superstitious herbs' at his door or made 'either plum pottage or nativity pies'. Hence the nickname of the ensuing disturbances – 'The Plum Pottage Riots'.

The Reverend Aldy of St Andrew's Church preached on Christmas Day in defiance of this proclamation, but the Puritans tried to disrupt the service by making noisy demonstrations outside the church. Twelve shops opened and the Royalists damaged their goods and tried to persuade them to close. Mayor Bridge toured Canterbury encouraging shopkeepers to open up and when receiving a rude answer from one, struck him in the face and then was himself seized upon and thrown

Cartoon of Old Father Christmas in the seventeenth century being respectively welcomed by Royalists and turned away by Puritans.

into the gutter. This led to further assaults on Puritans; their windows were broken and their goods thrown about the streets. The Royalists barricaded St George's Gate, Burgate and Wincheap Gate with timber and their watchword was, 'For God, King Charles and Kent'.

On Boxing Day, the Mayor set a small armed guard under the leadership of Captain White, a barber, to watch the gate, and he shot one of the crowd for calling him a 'Roundhead', which caused a fresh riot. The citizens came forth with clubs and assaulted and imprisoned Captain White and attacked the house of the

St George's Gate, Canterbury.

Mayor, who had fled. The citizens obtained the keys to the prison and set their own guards over the city. By 27 December, the Royalist insurgents had increased to over 1,000 and they took control of the Town Hall and with it a supply of arms and powder. When the Sheriff intervened to try to rescue Captain White, 'he was knocked down and his head fearfully broke; it was God's mercy his brains were not beat out'. Other Puritans were attacked, including Thomas Harris, who was described as 'a busy prating fellow'.

Eventually, the Justices of the Peace persuaded the citizens to lay down their arms on condition that no retribution would be taken against them. However, the Mayor brought in 3,000 Roundhead soldiers, who damaged the city gates and walls and imprisoned the Justices in Leeds Castle for two months. Some of the rioters were imprisoned and tried, including the poet Francis

Lovelace, who wrote his famous poem 'To Althea From Prison' there, with its famous line 'Stone walls do not a prison make'.

The jury found the defendants not guilty and organised a petition requesting that King and Parliament should settle 'the Peace both of Church and Commonwealth'. The reaction of Parliament to this petition was to threaten to hang two petitioners from each parish and this led to a general Royalist uprising in Kent, defeated in a pitched battle at Maidstone. Not until the restoration of the 'Merry Monarch' Charles II in 1660 could Christmas be properly celebrated. Appropriately, the King landed in Kent, greeted symbolically by the erection of two maypoles at Deal – maypoles had also been banned by the Puritan Parliament.

Christmas Superstitions

Sidney Bredgar, in an article in the *Invicta Magazine* entitled 'Some Curious Old Customs in East Kent', mentions two traditions which show belief in the veneration of the birth of Jesus by the natural world:

> The belief still survives that, on Christmas Eve, exactly at the hour of midnight, a certain rose slowly opens and re-closes its petals to salute the birthday of our Lord; and some of the old country folk also believe that, at the same

Christmas gambols or a kiss under the mistletoe.

moment, and for the same purpose, all the sheep in the
meadows turn and bow towards the East.

The second of these traditions seems to be a Kent par-
allel tradition to that in Dorset, referred to by Thomas
Hardy in *Tess of the D'Urbervilles* and his beautiful poem
'The Oxen', of the farm beasts kneeling at midnight on
Christmas Eve.

An interesting custom last documented at Walmer was
to give cocks extra food on Christmas Eve so that they
would spot any evil spirits abroad. Their special cake,
made of fat and grain, was called 'the Christmas Sheaf'
and is apparently still fed to birds on the local duck pond
on Christmas Eve.

The Sundridge Band – Sevenoaks News Interview with Tom Muggleton, 1936

In 1936, Tom Muggleton of Spring Cottagee, Sundridge, a trained Army musician, recalled his youthful experiences with his band touring the big houses north-west of Sevenoaks in the *Sevenoaks News*:

> It was Boxing Day morning fifty years ago, when we set out with our band to tour Brasted and Sundridge. After calling at Brasted Place we made our way to Coombe Bank, then the residence of Count de Baillet. Unfortunately, the Countess had a strong aversion to drums, and, what proved more unfortunate was the fact that the band did not know this.
>
> We were playing a little waltz, when the bass drummer, who should have been beating softly, suddenly began to bang his drum vigorously. I looked up at him, but before I had time to stop him, a tall lady swept past me and with a folded umbrella whacked that drummer such a resounding smack on the side of his head that his cap was sent flying into the middle of the ring of musicians. With 'Stop it, will you?' the lady turned and vanished through the front door. It was the Countess.
>
> …However, the band received a subscription on leaving and went away thanking their lucky stars that events had not turned out worse.

Village choir rehearsing a Christmas anthem.

Fortunately, their reception at other ports of call was not quite so robust. Tramping their way into Chevening, they visited the residence of Earl Stanhope, where their efforts were rewarded with tankards of good old ale brewed at the home with tasty Devonshire cheese, and a good subscription. That gave us a better heart after our previous damper. At Ide Hill and Chipstead their receptions were equally as warm.

...From Ide Hill, the band journeyed down to Brasted Chart, finishing at Heverswood, the residence of Mrs Henderson. Here the butler handed them a subscription, but on inspecting the players in their green uniforms he said, 'Well, this is the most respectable litle band I have ever seen. I am sure you must play nicely, but I am sorry to say I cannot hear you, as I am stone deaf !!!'

(*Sevenoaks News* 24 December 1936 – interview with Tom Muggleton of Spring Cottage, Sundridge.)

Kentish Carols

The Seven Joys of Mary

'The Seven Joys' was once a very popular carol in Kent, and derives from the medieval adoration of the Virgin. The 'seven joys of Mary' were said to compensate for the seven sorrowful events in her life and included the Annunciation; Visitation; Nativity of Jesus; Adoration of the Three Kings; finding of the boy Jesus in the Temple; the Resurrection; and the Assumption. There is a distinctive Kentish version of 'The Seven Joys of Mary' said in 1889 in the Kent Archaeological Society's 'Notes and Queries' to be 'a favourite with the Gravesend juveniles just before and at Christmas, when it may be repeatedly heard in the town and suburbs'. The Kent version is unusual in having Jesus 'ride above the sun' in the first verse and wearing the crucifix instead of being on it in verse six.

'The Seven Joys of Mary'
(Gravesend version)

The First good joy that Mary had
It was the joy of one,
To see her own son Jesus,
To ride above the sun,

REFRAIN

To ride above the sun, good man,
And blessed may He be;
Both Father, Son, and Holy Ghost,
To all eternity.

The next good joy that Mary had,
It was the joy of two,
To see her own son Jesus,
To make the lame to go.

The next good joy that Mary had,
It was the joy of three.
When that her own son Jesus
Did make the blind to see.

The next good joy that Mary had,
It was the joy of four,
To see her own son Jesus,
To read the Scriptures o'er.

Nativity scene.

The next good joy that Mary had,
It was the joy of five,
To see her own son Jesus,
To raise the dead to life.

The next good joy that Mary had,
It was the joy of six,
To see her own son Jesus,
To wear the Crucifix.

The next good joy that Mary had
It was the joy of seven,
To see her own son Jesus,
To wear the crown of heaven.

The same Notes and Queries source also refers (in a letter dated 29 December 1888) to a Gravesend version of the carol 'I Saw Three Ships' entitled 'The Sunny Bank':

The Sunny Bank

As I sat on a sunny bank,
A sunny bank, a sunny bank,
As I sat on a sunny bank,
On Christmas day in the morning.

I spied three ships come sailing by,
Come sailing by, come sailing by,
I spied three ships come sailing by,
On Christmas day in the morning.

And who should be with these three ships,
With these three ships, with these three ships.
And who should be with these three ships,
But Joseph and his fair lady.

Then he did whistle, she did sing,
And all the bells on the earth did ring,
For joy that our Saviour was born,
On Christmas day in the morning.

New Year Gifts at Court

The giving of gifts at midwinter stems from both the
Roman and pagan Anglo-Saxon cultures. Surviving
records for England in general, and Kent in particular, for medieval, Elizabethan and Jacobean times, are
mainly for the upper classes and show that the giving
of New Year gifts was far more prevalent than the
giving of Christmas gifts. But Geoffrey Chaucer, a
page in the household of Elizabeth, Countess of Ulster
(wife of Prince Lionel) was given 20s 'for necessaries at
Christmas' in December 1367. His wife Phillipa, when
in service with John of Gaunt, was given a New Year's
gift of a silver-gilt buttoner with six buttons in 1373 and
she received silver-gilt cups for New Year's gifts in 1380-
82. Geoffrey was also working for Gaunt at this time to
be with his wife (Gaunt later married Philippa's sister)

Penshurst Place. (Geoff Doel)

and a comic remark in *The Canterbury Tales* suggests that the Chaucers (or possibly Chaucer after his wife's death) lived at Greenwich for a period.

In the Tudor and Jacobean periods it was customary for the monarch to exchange New Year gifts with leading subjects. In 1532, Anne Boleyn, whose Kentish family seat was Hever Castle and whose mother and sister were believed to have preceded her as Henry Vlll's mistresses, gave Henry an exotic set of richly decorated Pyrenean boar spears as a New Year's gift. Henry gave Anne a matching set of hangings for her room and bed in cloth of gold, cloth of silver and richly embroidered crimson satin.

Sir Philip Sidney of Penshurst Place – celebrated poet, soldier and statesman – was at court on New Year's Day

1578 and gave Queen Elizabeth 'a cambric chemise, wrought with black work, and a pair of ruffs set with spangles'. The Queen gave Sir Philip 'some gilt plate, weighing twenty-two ounces'. Sir Philip Sidney later offended the Queen by opposing the suggested marriage alliance between Elizabeth and the Duc d'Anjou. Sir Philip's New Year gifts to the Queen in 1581 were thus highly symbolic – 'a whip, to show that he had been scourged, a chain, to chain him to Her Majesty, and a heart of gold, to show that he was now entirely hers'. It is probably on this occasion that Queen Elizabeth reciprocated by giving Sir Philip the portrait of herself by Zucchero which still hangs at Penshurst Place.

Lady Anne Clifford was very friendly with Queen Anne, wife of James I, and her diary survives for part of the time she lived at Knole House in Knole Park near Sevenoaks. She records in her diary for December 1616, 'Upon the 31st I sent Thomas Woodgate with a sweet bag to the Queen for a New Year's gift, & a Standish to Mrs Hanns, both cost me about 16 or 17 pounds.' The diary records for January 1619 that on 1 January, 'I sent the Queen a New Year's Gift, a cloth of silver Cushion embroidered richly with the King of Denmark's Arms, and all one with stripes of Tent Stitch'.

The diaries do not record any reciprocal gifts sent by the Queen; the Queen was seriously ill in January 1619 and the diary records her death in March and Lady Anne's presence as a mourner in the funeral in May.

Becket's Last Christmas
BY HERBERT OF BOSHAM AND GERVASE OF CANTERBURY

Becket's biographer, Herbert of Bosham, was born in Bosham in 1120 and was known to be a part of Thomas à Becket's household by 1162 as an assistant, advisor on scripture and companion, and he remained loyal to Becket to the end. Becket sent him to the Continent just before his murder; he was neglected by former friends of Becket after the latter's death and died in 1190.

Kent was fortunate to have the richest and most popular healing shrine in Britain, which attracted massive revenue to the county and gave it an international reputation – that of St Thomas à Becket (d. 1170), a martyred Archbishop of Canterbury. Chaucer's *The Canterbury Tales*, written in the 1380s, are about a group of people heading for the shrine. Becket was claimed to cure every kind of disease and his shrine was run as a tremendously successful business by the monks of Canterbury Cathedral for many years until in 1538 Henry VIII had the gold-and-gem-encrusted shrine dismantled, confiscated the wealth of the cathedral and destroyed all the relics. The story of Becket's bloody end in his own sanctuary cathedral in 1170 at the hands of four of Henry II's liegemen, Reginald Fitzurse, William de Tracy, Richard le Breton and Hugh de Moreville, is scarcely less riveting than the record of Henry II's subsequent enforced humiliation at the hands of the Church. Barefooted,

bareheaded and in his shift, he walked to Canterbury
Cathedral before the stunned townspeople, after which
he endured a whipping at the hands of bishop and abbot
and eighty of Becket's monk community before Becket's
mutilated body (at that date enshrined in the crypt):

> On the day of our Lord's Nativity, which was, if I mis-
> take not, about the twenty-seventh day after our arrival in
> England, the archbishop mounted the pulpit and preached
> to the people. At the end of his sermon he predicted that
> the time of his departure drew near and that shortly he
> would be taken from them. And when he said this concern-
> ing his departure, tears rather than words burst from him.
> Likewise the hearts of his hearers were beyond measure
> moved with grief and contrition, so that you might have
> seen and heard in every corner of the church weeping and
> lamentation, and the people murmuring among themselves,
> 'Father, why do you desert us so soon, and to whom do you
> leave us so desolate?' For these were no wolves but sheep
> who knew the voice of their shepherd and grieved when
> they heard him say that he would so soon leave this world…
> The service ended, the archbishop, who had shown him-
> self so devout at the Lord's table that day, afterwards made
> merry, as was his wont, at the table of this world. Moreover,
> as it was the feast of the Nativity, although a Friday, he ate
> meat, as on other days, thereby demonstrating that on such a
> festival it was more religious to eat than to abstain.
>
> On the morrow of the Nativity, that is, on the feast of
> the blessed martyr Stephen, he called apart the disciple
> who wrote these things, and said to him, 'I have arranged

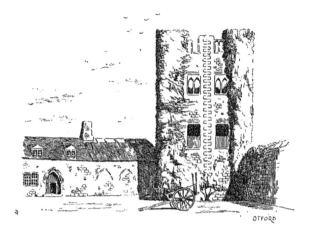

OTFORD

Otford Palace.

to send you to our lord, the king of the French, to our venerable brother, the archbishop of Sens, and to other princes of that land, to tell them what you have seen and heard concerning this peace, how for us it is a peace which is no peace, but rather turmoil and confusion.' The disciple, unable to restrain his tears, made answer, 'Holy father, why have you done this? Why act in this way? I know for certain that I shall see you in the flesh no more. I had determined to stay faithfully at your side, truly, so it seems to me, you are seeking to deprive me of the fruit of your consummation, me who have hitherto continued with you in your temptations; nor shall I be, as now I see, a companion of your glory, who have been partner in your pain.' Then said the archbishop amid a flood of tears, 'Not so, my son, not so; you will not be deprived of the fruit, if you fulfil your father's commands and follow his counsel. Nevertheless, what you have said is indeed true, that you will see me in the flesh no more. Yet I wish you to go, especially since the king holds you in greater suspicion than the others, where the cause of the Church is at stake.' So, on the second day after Christmas, being the feast of St John the Evangelist, in the darkness of the night, for fear of being waylaid, I took my leave of my father with lamentation and many tears.

…When the three excommunicated bishops had incited the king to a fury that should be detested by all future generations, so that he was like an oven heated by cooks, unable to contain the fire, openly, in the presence of everyone, and particularly in the presence of his own people in the court, whom he had nourished and upon whom he had conferred honours and many benefits, he complained about the archbishop as though he were an enemy inflamed by wrath, speaking in a funereal voice, he often cursed those whom he had nourished, whom he had favoured and were indebted to him for their income, for not having avenged the wrongs done to him by the archbishop, who was disturbing him and his kingdom, and sought to undermine his authority and oust him from power. Having heard him repeatedly rage in this manner, four knights of the court decided, on the basis of what they heard him say, thought that they might ingratiate themselves with the king if they killed the archbishop; thus they took an oath to kill the archbishop. I have taken care to insert their names in this history, that they may be eternally damned: Hugo of Morville, Reginald the son of Ursus, William of Tracy, and

Saltwood Castle. (Geoff Doel)

the fourth was Richard Brito. These soldiers of the court, the king's men, although base, were certainly noblemen, well known for the honours they had earned, and leaders among the leaders. These four conspirators immediately set out for England.

...They arrived at the agreed upon place, Saltwood Castle, six miles from Canterbury, which the king had promised by oath to restore to the archbishop, in possession of the church of Canterbury...Throughout the night in the castle they plotted the murder of the archbishop, until the next day, which was the fourth day of the birth of the Lord, the day of the sacrifice of the Innocents, they came to Canterbury.

First the four previously mentioned soldiers haugh-tily approached the chamber in which the archbishop

was seated, towards the close of day…asking if he had absolved the king's bishops whom he had removed from office and excommunicated. When he graciously replied that he could not and should not dissolve bonds tied by the authority of his lord the Pope, furious with him, they immediately left, collected their men in the garden, and clothed themselves in the armour of the devil.

…When the knights had armed themselves and collected their supporters, with swords and clubs, they proceeded to throng through the windows of the palace, since the doors had been shut, out of fright, by members of our household. Those who were seated with the archbishop in his chamber, hearing the crowd and noise outside, became frightened, for good reasons, and advised the archbishop to take refuge in the most sacred and safest place, that is, the church. After he had resisted several times, fearless in the face of death, at last they managed to force him to enter the church.

…Some of his men, when he had entered the church, soon shut and locked the gates of the cathedral. The murderous soldiers with their supporters, armed with swords and clubs, followed the archbishop on foot, and when they reached the doors of the church, they shouted loudly for the doors to be opened. After a short delay, they set about attacking the doors with iron machines they had prepared. (Becket) heard the noise and clamour at the gates of the church, and he ordered that they be opened immediately, adding that it was not appropriate to turn a church into a castle. When the doors were opened, the murderers rushed in immediately, and one of them cried out: 'Where is the false imposter.' But to this Becket said nothing. 'Where is the archbishop?' he said. And Becket said, 'I am he, what do you want? And he said loudly, 'That you die, that you live no longer.' And he said: 'And I am prepared to give up my life for my God and for the freedom of the church.'

But marvellous to relate, this singularly great warrior of God, singularly magnificent, who had entered the choir, which is reached by a ladder, before the executioners had entered the church, had already climbed the seventh octave step; as soon as he saw swords drawn in the church, he ran quickly to meet them. Not the messenger of his hard death, not the deadly word, not the metal drawn forth for his death, could call him back from the confrontation. And what added to the wonder and shock, he vigorously condemned the gladiators who had entered the church in such a disorderly, profane fashion, seizing one of them with his hand, and striking him so powerfully that he almost knocked him to the ground. This was William of Tracy, as he later confessed about himself.

…Without seeking a moment's grace, without asking for any favour, without asking for a delay, driven by priestly zeal and by the love of justice, he provoked rather than placated the wrath of those who were enraged against him. O powerful handoff a daring athlete, oh strength of the man, oh constancy of the martyr, oh purity of soul! Priest and sacrifice, he stood imperiously among the murderers, while they surrounded him with swords drawn. In their midst the priest fulfilled the office of priest, he did not try to calm the gladiators, nor did he humble himself, but he argued with them and upbraided them.

The final details of the murder are supplied by Gervase of Canterbury:

After they had rushed through the open door, they separated from each other, Fitz-Urse turning to the left, while the three others took to the right. The archbishop had already ascended a few steps, when Fitz-Urse, as he hurried onwards, asked one whom he met, 'Where is the archbishop?' Hearing this, he turned round on the step, and with a slight motion of the head, he was the first to answer, 'Here am I, Reginald. I have conferred many a benefit on you, Reginald; and do you now come to me with arms in your hands?' 'You shall soon find that out,' was the reply. 'Are you not that notorious traitor to the king?' And, laying hold on his pall, he said, 'Depart hence;' and he struck the pall with his sword. The archbishop replied, 'I am no traitor, nor will I depart, wretched man!' and he plucked the fringe of his pall from out the knight's hand. The other repeated the words, 'Flee hence! The reply was, 'I will not flee; here your malice shall be satisfied.' At these words the assassin stepped back, as if smitten by a blow. In the meantime the other three assailants had arrived; and they exclaimed, 'Now you shall die!' 'If,' said the archbishop, ' you seek my life, I forbid you, under the threat of an anathema, from touching any one of my followers. As for me, I willingly embrace death, provided only that the church obtain liberty and peace at the price of my blood.' When he had said these words, he stretched forth his head to the blows of the murderers. Fitz-Urse hastened forward, and with his whole strength planted a blow upon the extended head; and

Eastbridge Hospital, Canterbury, which accommodated pilgrims visiting the shrine of St Thomas.

he cried out, as if in triumph over his conquered enemy, 'Strike! strike! Goaded on by the author of confusion, these butchers, adding wound to wound, dashed out his brains; and one of them following up the martyr (who at this time was either in the act of falling, or had already fallen), struck the pavement with his sword but the point of the weapon broke off short. They now returned through the cloister, crying out, 'Knights of the king, let us go; he is dead!

…This blessed martyr suffered death in the ninth year of his patriarchate, on 29 December, being the third day of the week, AD 1170, while the monks were singing their vespers. His dead body was removed and placed in the shrine before the altar of Christ. On the morrow it was carried by the monks and deposited in a tomb of marble within the crypt. Now, to speak the truth – that which I saw with my eyes, and handled with my hands – he wore hair-cloth next his skin, then stamin, over that a black cowl, then the white cowl in which he was consecrated; he also wore his tunic and dalmatic, his chasuble, pall, and mitre; lower down, he had drawers of sack-cloth, Andover these others of linen; his socks were of wool, and he had on sandals.

From *I Am Christmas*
BY JOHN RYMAN

We began our Christmas selection with John Ryman's diatribe against Advent, so it seems appropriate to end with his reluctant farewell to long Christmas celebrations that he has apparently enjoyed in the company of the King in a nobleman's hall. He may indeed have recited his poem at the end of the festivities. These celebrations have ended, not at Twelfth Night, but at Candlemass (2 February). In Queen Elizabeth's court, the Christmas celebrations also continued until Candlemass and Robert Herrick, a seventeenth-century poet describes the removal of the Christmas decorations in his poem 'Ceremony Upon Candlemass Eve':

Down with the rosemary, and so
Down with the bays and mistletoe;

Monks or friars feasting.

> Down with the holly, ivy, all,
> Wherewith ye dress'd the Christmas Hall:
> That so the superstitious find
> No one least branch there left behind:
> For look, how many leaves there be
> Neglected, there (maids, trust to me)
> So many goblins you shall see.

As with the later Twelfth Night traditions it was unlucky to leave up decorations beyond the prescribed limit. John Ryman's sad farewell to Christmas includes a very modern sounding last line to each verse – 'Now have good day!':

> Here have I dwelled with more or lass
> From Hallowtide till Candelmas,
> And now must I from you hens pass;
> Now have good day!

I take my leve of king and knight,
And erl, baron, and lady bright;
To wilderness I must me dight; (dight = 'go')
Now have good day!

And at the good lord of this hall
I take my leve, and of gestes all;
Me think I here Lent doth call;
Now have good day!

'Pious Delight'.

And at every worthy officere,
Marshall, panter, and butlere
I tak my leve as for this yere;
Now have good day!

Another yere I trust I shall
Make mery in this hall,
If rest and peace in England fall;
Now have good day!

But oftentimes I have herd say
That he is loth to part away
That often biddeth 'Have good day!'
Now have good day!

Now fare ye well, all in fere,
Now fare ye well for all this yere;
Yet for my sake make ye good chere;
Now have good day!

BIBLIOGRAPHY

Books

Ackroyd, Peter, *Dickens* (London: Vintage, 1994).

Anon, *The Chronicles of Greenwich* , vol.1 (London: Hurst & Blackett, 1886).

Richard Barham, *The Ingoldsby Legends* (Edinburgh: Bentley & Son, 1885).

Bede, *Ecclesiastical History of the English People* (Harmonsdworth: Penguin, 1990).

Chaucer, Geoffrey, *The Canterbury Tales* (London: Penguin Popular Classics, 1996).

Clifford, D.J.H. (ed.) *The Diaries of Lady Anne Clifford* (Stroud: Sutton, 1990).

Coltman, P. (ed.) *The Diary of a Prison Governor* 1825 – 1890 (Kent County Council, August 1984).

Dickens, Charles, *Great Expectations* (London: Penguin, first serialised 1861, 1996).

Dickens, Charles, *The Pickwick Papers* (Harmondsworth: Penguin, 1972).

Dickens, Charles, 'The Seven Poor Travellers' from *The Christmas Stories* (London: J.M. Dent, 1996).

Dickens, Mamie, *My Father as I Recall Him* (The Roxburghe Press, 1897).

Doel, Fran & Geoff, *A Kent Christmas* (Stroud: Sutton, 1990, 1998).

Doel, Fran & Geoff, *Folklore of Kent* (Stroud: The History Press, 2003, 2009).

Doel, Fran & Geoff, *Mumming, Howling & Hoodening: Midwinter Rituals in Sussex, Kent and Surrey* (Rainham: Meresborough, 1992).

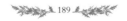

Fairfax, M.F.H.J., *Hunting reminiscences of H.W Selby Lowndes, Esq.*
(Blakeborough, 1926).

Glancy, Ruth, 'The Seven Poor Travellers' from *The Christmas Stories by
Charles Dickens* (Everyman Dickens, 1996).

Grew, B. D., *Some Considerations of a Prison Governor* (London: Herbert
Jenkins, 1958).

Harris, J. Rendel, *The Origin & Meaning of Apple Cults* (Manchester:
Manchester University Press and Longmans, 1917).

Hasted, Edward, *The History & Topographical Survey of the County of Kent*
(Canterbury: EP Publishing, 1797-1801, 1972).

Hutton, Ronald, *Stations of the Sun* (Oxford: Oxford University Press,
1996).

Lambarde, William, *Perambulation of Kent* (Bath: Adams & Dart, 1570).

Maylam, Percy, *The Hooden Horse* (1909), ed. Lynn, Maylam & Doel
(Stroud: The History Press, 2009).

Monmouth, Geofrey, *History of the Kings of Britain* (Harmondsworth:
Penguin, 1966).

Parish & Shaw (aug. Alan Major) *A New Dictionary of Kent Dialect*
(Rainham: Meresborough, 1981).

Rowsby, P., *The Diary of Eva Knatchbull-Hugessen 1873-1875* (Kent Archive
Office, 1986).

Smithers, David Waldron, *A History of Knockolt* (Speldhurst: Dragonfly
Press, 1991).

Stevenson, Joseph, *The Church Historians of England* (London: Seely's,
1853).

Journals & Newspapers

Doel, Fran & Geoff, 'Ken Thompson – a Kentish Man and his Songs',
English Dance & Song, 54/2, Summer, 1992.

Herne Bay Press, 26 December 1942 & 19 December 1944.

Kent County Examiner & Ashford Chronicle, 20 December 1895.

Kentish Express and Ashford News, 29 December 1917.

Kent Post, 1750, 1751, 1752.

Sevenoaks Chronicle, Westerham Courier & Kentish Advertiser, Friday 22
December 1944.

Tuesday Express, 28 December 1915.

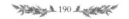

Other titles published by The History Press

A Devonshire Christmas

MIKE HOLGATE

Explore the rich heritage of Christmas past in Devon with this varied collection of carols and customs, stories, folklore and reminiscences. With extracts from a diverse range of sources, including novels, journals and diaries, this delightful anthology features seasonal extracts from writers with local connections such as Charles Dickens, Henry Williamson and Eden Phillpotts.

978 0 7524 5170 1

Christmas Past in Sussex

FRAN & GEOFF DOEL

Providing readers with a seasonal anthology of the county, this collection of Sussex carols and customs, seasonal recipes and literary tales, re-examines the rich heritage of Christmas past from around the county. It features Christmas disasters, such as the Lewes avalanche, to well-known seasonal songs – such as Good King Wenceslas.

978 0 7524 3670 8

Folklore of Kent

FRAN & GEOFF DOEL

Kent boasts a plethora of characterising traditions which reflect the curious history and geography of the area – it has the longest coastline of any English county was the base for much maritime activity. This book covers topics such as seasonal customs including harvest traditions; drama; witchcraft; saints and holy wells; and the background and songs surrounding fruit and hop-growing.

978 0 7524 2628 0

Percy Maylam's The Kent Hooden Horse

RICHARD MAYLAM, MICK LYNN & GEOFF DOEL

In 1909, Canterbury antiquarian Percy Maylam published his research and remarkable photographs of the fascinating Kent tradition of the Hooden Horse and also a famous essay on the Kent custom of Gavelkind. Percy's great-nephew Richard Maylam, together with Mick Lynn and Geoff Doel, has worked to make Percy Maylam's text available to a new generation of potential hoodeners and their audiences.

978 07524 4997 5

Visit our website and discover thousands of other History Press books.

www.thehistorypress.co.uk